LARRY'S FAVORITE CHOCOLATE CAKE

A Serious Comedy in Two Acts

by

KENT R. BROWN

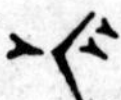

Dramatic Publishing
Woodstock, Illinois • London, England • Melbourne, Australia

*** NOTICE ***

Printed in the United States of America

(LARRY'S FAVORITE CHOCOLATE CAKE)

Cover design by Susan Carle

ISBN 0-87129-649-7

In February, 1995, *LARRY'S FAVORITE CHOCOLATE CAKE* received a developmental reading at Arkansas Rep under the guidance of Artistic Director Cliff Baker. The cast included Ron Aulgur, Steve Wilkerson, Graham Gordy, Frances Kemp, Richard Glover, Jennifer Catney and Vivian Morrison.

A second reading was held in March at the BoarsHead Theatre in Lansing, Michigan under the direction of Ed Menta. The cast featured John Peakes, Carmen Decker, Buck Schirner, Bethany Smith, Peter Ruvolo, Dana Munshaw and Greg Bodine.

In 1996, *LARRY'S FAVORITE CHOCOLATE CAKE* was a Finalist in the Norfolk Southern Festival of New Works, and received its premiere production at the Mill Mountain Theatre, Roanoke, Virginia; Jere Hodgin, Executive/Artistic Director. Doug Zschiegner directed the production which featured Michael Mansfield, Vincent Wares, Dorothy B. Johnson, Dawn Westbrook, Shaun Mabry, Jody Wade, Bruce Barton and Eddie Collins.

LARRY'S FAVORITE CHOCOLATE CAKE

A Play in Two Acts
For 4-5 Men and 3-4 Women

CHARACTERS

SPARKY . . . . Larry's father
DORIS . . . . Larry's mother
LARRY mid-40s
MICHELLE . . . . Larry's wife
KEVIN . . . . Larry and Michelle's teenage son
LORAINE . . . . Larry's office "companion"
(doubles as TRAVEL AGENT)
THE BOSS . . . . Larry's former employer
(doubles as THE LOVER)
TRAVEL AGENT . . . . an effective saleswoman
THE LOVER . . . . Michelle's wannabe office lover

PROPS ASSISTANT, TV ANNOUNCER, CHEEVES THE BUTLER, and THE DOCTOR: These characters should be shared by "all purpose" actors (male and female) with specific assignments left to the discretion of the director.

TIME

The present, the past, and LARRY's imagination.

SETTING

A wing-back chair, a small table and a telephone are the only permanent pieces in what is otherwise a bare space. Isolated items such as a telephone stand, a bed, a rowboat, an additional chair and so on, will make their appearance later.

SOUND EFFECTS

Use sparingly: boat whistles, car horns, Big Ben perhaps, the ticking of a clock, and so on.

ACT ONE

AT RISE: *LIGHTS reveal SPARKY "conducting" a classical Beethoven piece. He is awash in the spirit of the music.*

The telephone rings. SPARKY continues "conducting" the music. He audibly underscores the piece with a "da-de-dum-dum-de" now and then. After a moment DORIS enters from the "hallway" carrying a suitcase. She crosses to the "front door" and sets the suitcase down.

DORIS. Sparky! The telephone! Answer the telephone, sweetheart. I've got my hands full here. *(Exits to the "kitchen.")*

SPARKY *(hearing the telephone but still absorbed in the music. Calling offstage).* Doris, the telephone's ringing. I'll get it. *(But he remains absorbed in the music.)*

(DORIS appears from the "kitchen" with an apron around her waist and moves toward the "hallway.")

DORIS. Sparky! Answer the damn phone. I only have two hands! Share the wear, sweetheart, dinner's in the pot. *(DORIS exits to the "hallway.")*

SPARKY *(answering the telephone).* Hello? Who is this? *(SPARKY's attention remains focused on the music.)* Make it quick, will you? Dinner's in the pot and I've got Beethoven by the throat here! Ta-da! Da-da-dum-dum-dum-dum-de-dum!

(DORIS enters from the "hallway" carrying another suitcase and two carry-on bags with straps. She places the items by the "front door.")

DORIS. Is it the travel agent, Sparky? Are there any problems? Is everything all right?

SPARKY *(into the telephone).* Is everything all right? What? Speak up. *(To DORIS.)* I don't think everything's all right.

DORIS. What do you mean everything's not all right? Give me that phone! *(DORIS takes the telephone from SPARKY.)* What is this about problems? We aren't paying a fortune for any problems. We're paying for the trip of a lifetime! Everything's all set out. But if you have some personal problems you want to get off your chest you can come over and have a little chicken soup with Sparky and spill your guts. We're very good listeners. Just take the Jackson Grove exit off I-64 North, you know where that is, I'm sure, then a…

(As DORIS begins giving directions and SPARKY continues "conducting" the music, LARRY enters carrying two suitcases and a backpack with a trenching tool, a poncho, an old baseball mitt and a mess kit attached to it. He is wearing a rumpled business suit and carrying a briefcase. The total effect is somewhat surreal.)

DORIS *(continuing).* …sharp left at the 7-11 with the Slurpee on the window.

SPARKY. Then right at the Texaco!

DORIS. Then right at the Texaco, left at the Wal-Mart…

LARRY. Mom? Dad?

DORIS. …left again at the Bingo Palace. Oops, hang on now! Sparky, do you go three lights after the McDonald's or four…*(SPARKY holds up three fingers.)* Three! Got it now. We're back on the trail. Three lights…*(LARRY puts down his baggage and exits.)*…and keep the cemetery on your right, and the auto salvage yard on your left. Now, a half mile past the Green Parrot sign you'll see an old blue Oldsmobile 88 sitting up on blocks.

(LARRY re-enters with several more items including a small tricycle.)

DORIS. And there you'll be. 6743 Paradise Lane. On the corner. We'll be waiting. *(DORIS completes her directions, hangs up the telephone, and begins to cross to the "kitchen.")* Shape up, Sparky. We've got company for dinner. Then we finish packing, make out the mail card and we're off! *(DORIS sees LARRY completely surrounded now by his gear. SPARKY continues "conducting.")*

LARRY. Hi, Mom!

DORIS. Larry?

LARRY. Hi!

DORIS. Sparky? Sparky! *(DORIS's insistent tone "shuts off" the music. SPARKY continues vocalizing for a moment before realizing there is no music.)*

SPARKY. What happened to the—

DORIS. It's Larry.

SPARKY. Larry? No, dear. It's Beethoven.

DORIS. It's Larry. He's here.

SPARKY. Where?

DORIS *(pointing to LARRY)*. There!

SPARKY *(seeing LARRY, he, too, is visibly surprised. SPARKY and DORIS exchange looks)*. Son? Is that you?

LARRY. Hi, Dad. That old Oldsmobile 88 sure was something, wasn't it? I'll get right to it in the morning. Some good old elbow grease and I'll have it looking good as new again.

DORIS. Well, this is a big surprise. We were expecting the—

LARRY. Yeah, hey, me, too. Big surprise here, let me tell you.

SPARKY. Is it really you, son?

LARRY. Sure is, Dad.

DORIS. It's Larry, Daddy.

LARRY. I've brought a few things with me.

DORIS *(looking behind LARRY to see if someone else is there)*. Where is, uh, did you bring…

LARRY. Michelle?

DORIS. Michelle, yes, Michelle. Is she with—

LARRY. Uh, no, she couldn't make it this trip.

SPARKY. Oh, that's too bad.

DORIS. We never see enough of her.

LARRY. Yes, well, she's very busy.

SPARKY. What about…did you bring, uh…

DORIS. Kevin.

SPARKY. Of course. Kevin. Slipped my mind for a second there.

LARRY. Uh, no. Kevin's home, too. With Michelle. Michelle and Kevin are both home.

DORIS. Oh. Both home. I see.

SPARKY. Both home, eh?

DORIS. But you're here. With your suitcases and camping gear.

LARRY. Yeah, guess I am. *(There is a period of extended awkwardness.)*

DORIS. What's the matter, Larry? A mother always knows when her child's in trouble.

SPARKY *(in a "You can tell us anything, son" tone).* A father knows, too, Larry, but not as much as a mother knows...so 'fess up, son.

LARRY. Uh, yeah. Well, you're right, Mom. Look, uh—this is...I bet this looks sort of strange. I don't know how to tell you this.

SPARKY. Go ahead, son. Just open your mouth and let her rip! We can take it, can't we, Mother?

DORIS *(a bit wary).* That depends.

LARRY. I've come home.

SPARKY. Is that it? Is that all? You've come home?

LARRY. Yes.

SPARKY. Well, that wasn't so hard, was it, son? Larry's come home, Mother.

DORIS. So I heard.

LARRY. I'm back.

SPARKY *(not comprehending the implications of what LARRY has just said).* Mother, Larry's back! Isn't that wonderful?

DORIS. Back? What do you mean...back?

LARRY. Back. Like...come back home...back in.

DORIS. Back in? Like...move back in?

LARRY. Yes. Like move back in.

SPARKY. Back in where, son?

LARRY. Here. This house. With you and Mom. Home again.

SPARKY. Home again? Like come back home again?

DORIS. Now? Here?

SPARKY. Tonight?

LARRY. Here I am! Back.

DORIS *(supportive but cautious).* For how long are you back?

LARRY. I don't know yet. For a while. A visit.

DORIS. A short visit? Then back home to—

SPARKY. Michelle and Kevin! *(SPARKY gives the "thumbs-up" gesture to DORIS.)*

LARRY. Well, maybe not a short visit.

DORIS. Not a short visit.

LARRY. No.

DORIS. Longer than a short visit? *(LARRY nods and smiles.)*

SPARKY. Oh, oh.

LARRY *(looking about the room)*. Oh, it feels so good to be back. The old memories. When times were simpler. No cares. No troubles. Just take out the trash and be in by ten. A feeling of safety and love. I've been gone too long. Mom! Dad! *(It's now time for the family "hug." LARRY opens his arms and moves toward SPARKY and DORIS. SPARKY and DORIS exchange "Do you think he really means to move back in" looks. As LARRY gets closer, SPARKY retreats behind the wing-back chair. LARRY then pursues DORIS who retreats as well. The "chase" increases in tempo, but no one actually hugs anyone. An effort should be made to elongate this segment. The characters could be caught in a series of "freeze frames" as they work to align themselves in this strange familial dance. "Slow motion" could also be used, underscored by chase music. When the "chase" ceases, all three catch their breath.)*

SPARKY. Whoa! That was a heck of a ride, eh, Big Guy?

LARRY. Sure was, Dad. That was great. Just like cowboys and Indians. *(Slowly, LARRY extends his hand. SPARKY shakes it. Then LARRY steps in and embraces his father.)* Dad! Oh, boy. *(LARRY then goes to DORIS and embraces her.)* Mom! You look great!

DORIS *(during the hug)*. Have you gained weight?

LARRY. A little, I guess, yeah. All the stress. Overtime.

DORIS. You look tired.

LARRY. Yeah, a bit. Deadlines. Traffic. Taxes. The usual.

SPARKY. Got to take care of yourself, son. I can't take care of myself anymore so Mother blocks downfield for me, don't you, Mother?

DORIS. Have to protect my investment. *(DORIS and SPARKY look at the items LARRY has brought with him.)*

SPARKY. What's all this stuff, son? Is this a tricycle?

LARRY. Yeah, that's Kevin's old tricycle.

DORIS. What do you need a tricycle for? Thought you had a car.

LARRY. Thought I could feel what it's like to be a little kid again.

DORIS. Why? You're a big person now.

LARRY. I know that, Mom. But it's not fun being a big person.

DORIS. Whoever said it was?

LARRY. Well I just thought I'd pull back a bit, take a breath.

DORIS. You're having trouble breathing, too?

LARRY. No, Mom. It's just an expression. I mean—

SPARKY *(hefting one of the suitcases)*. These suitcases are bulging at the seams, son.

DORIS. Sparky, your back!

LARRY. They're the Great Books, Dad.

SPARKY *(hefting another of the suitcases)*. The great and heavy books, you mean. Can't be great if they're not heavy, eh, son?

LARRY. That's right, Dad.

DORIS. And what about this camping gear?

SPARKY. Larry's going to climb Mt. Everest, Mother.

LARRY. Actually, Dad, I thought we might camp out in the back yard like we used to. You know, just the two of us. Cook marshmallows. Look at the sky. Read the Great Books. Talk about sex.

DORIS *(to SPARKY)*. Didn't you talk to Larry about sex, Sparky?

SPARKY. I'm sure I said something about it, dear.

LARRY. Look, I just need to relax a bit. Drop my guard. Think things out. Have some milk and cookies, you know? Touch bases with you.

SPARKY. I'm a little too old to play catch, son, but I'll give it a try.

DORIS. I don't think he means baseball, Sparky.

LARRY. I know this must come as a big surprise, just walking in on you like this.

DORIS. You're right there, son.

LARRY. But things seem to snowball all the time...and my job...and Michelle, Kevin. All of a sudden everything's falling off the plate.

SPARKY. Well, scoop it up off the floor, son, and slap it right back on the plate.

LARRY. It's too much. I'm feeling disconnected, fragmented. I'm losing my focus. I need to talk to you again.

SPARKY. That's what the telephone's for, son. Everybody knows that. Reach out, touch someone, then hang up.

LARRY. I know, Dad, but I don't think a phone call is going to do it this time. I'm feeling a little desperate here and... the phone is too—

SPARKY. We had a good talk the last time we called, didn't we, Mother?

LARRY. Actually, Michelle and I weren't doing that well and—

DORIS *(overlapping, trying to get her bearings)*. We did? Where was I?

LARRY *(overlapping)*. Dad, look, I'm in big trouble at work and I don't think Kevin is—

SPARKY. It was the sixth inning of the World Series, Mother, remember?

DORIS. I was in the kitchen! I'm always in the…

SPARKY *(overlapping)*. Bases were loaded!

LARRY *(trying to get their attention)*. I don't think my values are holding up. I don't think I'm doing the right—

SPARKY *(moving to the telephone and dialing)*. And I said to your mother, "I wonder if Larry is watching the Series."

DORIS. And I said…Good Lord, your dinner! Don't start without me. I'll be right back. *(DORIS exits to the "kitchen." The telephone is heard ringing offstage.)*

LARRY. Mom, will you please stay and listen! *(LARRY is beginning to feel overextended.)* I've come back for some answers. Can we talk now?

SPARKY *(calling offstage to DORIS)*. It's ringing, Mother!

LARRY. Dad, I'm standing right here! Look. Face to face, See? Can we…aw, damn! *(A telephone rolls onto the stage. In frustration LARRY crosses to the ringing telephone and answers it.)* Hello!

SPARKY. Hey, hey, there you are, Big Guy!

LARRY. Dad? Hi, Dad.

(DORIS appears with a soup ladle in her hand.)

DORIS. How is he? Is he eating all right?

LARRY. Everything OK, Dad?

SPARKY *(to DORIS)*. He's asking if everything's OK.

DORIS. Tell him we're still alive.

SPARKY. Your mother says we're still alive, son. That's good to know, isn't it?

MICHELLE *(from offstage)*. Larry, who is it? Larry—

DORIS. Let me talk to him. You always hog the telephone

SPARKY. Your mother wants to—

(MICHELLE enters with a coat over her arm.)

MICHELLE. We have to go now. Larry, I have to be back at work in—

LARRY *(overlapping with MICHELLE as DORIS reaches for the phone. In short: "Family Telephone Chaos")*. It's Dad. He wants to know if we're OK.

DORIS. Larry, it's your mother.

LARRY. Hi, Mom. Everything's fine here. Look, can I call you back tomorrow?

SPARKY *(yelling over DORIS's shoulder)*. Are you watching the Series, son?

MICHELLE *(overlapping)*. We're going to be late, Larry. We can't be late again.

LARRY. Did Dad say something, Mom?

DORIS. He wants to know if—

MICHELLE. Larry, please!

LARRY. We won't be late, Michelle.

SPARKY *(overlapping)*. What did he say?

DORIS *(taking full command of the telephone)*. You sound a little...are you all right?

LARRY. Well, we're in a hurry right now and—

DORIS. Daddy had his prostate checked. He's OK, but we're watching it.

SPARKY. Your mother doesn't mean we're actually watching it, son.

MICHELLE. Larry, I have obligations, too!

DORIS. And his hearing's going a bit off.

LARRY *(to MICHELLE)*. Give me a minute here, won't you? Mom says Dad's—

MICHELLE *(overlapping)*. Don't you want to make this work? I thought you wanted to—

SPARKY *(pulling the telephone closer to his ear. DORIS won't let go)*. I can't hear you too well, son. Your mother didn't pay the phone bill.

DORIS. I did, too, pay the phone bill!

MICHELLE. You agreed. You said you'd be there and—

LARRY *(to MICHELLE with frustration)*. It's been a while since we've talked. Please!

SPARKY. I know it has, son. What did you want to talk about?

LARRY. Uh, well, you called us, Dad.

SPARKY. Is that so?

MICHELLE. Are you going to tell them?

LARRY. Not over the phone.

DORIS. When are you coming to visit, Larry? It's been so long since your last—

MICHELLE. Then you call and cancel. It takes work to fix things, Larry. It was your—*(MICHELLE turns to exit.)*

LARRY. Dad, I've got to go, I'm sorry. *(MICHELLE stops and waits for LARRY.)*

SPARKY. Well, better to be going than not to be going. Your mother and I are going, that's for sure.

DORIS. We love you, son. Come by sometime and see us before we're gone and buried! *(DORIS exits to the "kitchen.")*

LARRY. I'm sorry, Dad. It's just that right now were having...you and Mom OK? You're not sick, are you? Brakes work OK? You rotating the tires like you taught me— That's important. Share the wear, remember? Love ya. I'll call you later! *(LARRY puts the telephone down. MICHELLE looks at LARRY for a moment, then turns and exits. The telephone rolls offstage. LARRY moves back into the "living room.")*

SPARKY *(hangs up the telephone)*. See, that was a good talk, wasn't it? When was that call again?

LARRY. Four years ago, I think, Dad.

SPARKY. Four years! My, my. Time moves on, doesn't it? Well, it's the communication age, son—We're on the cutting edge. We're opening envelopes, I think. Something with envelopes.

LARRY. Dad, please listen. I know I haven't been around much. I'm sorry for that. I've been real busy at work. Got two promotions last year, but I couldn't seem to—

SPARKY. Way to go, son! *(Calling offstage.)* Mother, Larry owns the company now.

LARRY. No, no, Dad, I'm the regional manager. I don't own the company.

SPARKY *(calling offstage)*. Larry lost the company, Mother.

LARRY. Dad, work seems to consume everything. Can't find time for...Michelle and...we're having problems. We've tried some counseling.

SPARKY. Counseling?

LARRY. Yes. I don't know if it's working.

SPARKY. What kind of counseling, son? You seem normal enough to me.

LARRY. Marriage counseling, Dad.

SPARKY. Oh, marriage counseling. One word of advice, son?

LARRY. Yes, sir, that's why I've come home.

SPARKY. Tell her you love her and give her a kiss before bed. That should wrap it up for you. Don't you love her?

LARRY. Yes, I do, Dad. I love Michelle very much, it's just that—

SPARKY. Have you been fishing in the wrong pond, son?

LARRY. Dad?

SPARKY. Life's little temptations, son. Big ones if you're lucky.

LARRY. I don't think I'm following you, Dad.

(LORAINE appears, seen only by LARRY.)

LORAINE. Are we all set for this afternoon, Larry? I've cleared my calendar.

SPARKY. Forbidden fruits, son. Tasty but forbidden.

LORAINE. I look forward to us every minute of the day, Larry. I can't wait. *(The LIGHTS fade out on LORAINE as she throws him a kiss.)*

LARRY. Uh, yes, I think I understand...I mean, no, I haven't.

SPARKY. I wasn't born yesterday, son. I'm a man, too, you know?

LARRY. Yes, sir. I knew you'd understand! I don't know how it—

SPARKY. Bills and more bills. Competition everywhere. Feel you need a...rest...a uh—

LARRY. An ear! Someone to listen who's not part of the problem.

SPARKY. It was more than an ear in my day, son, but I suppose times have changed. What I'm saying is when you've caught a good one, stuff her and put her up on the wall. That's what I did with your mother. Let the little ones get away, son. Keep your eyes on the big picture.

LARRY. Dad! I think I've lost the big picture. I don't seem to be able to make good decisions anymore. Sometimes I just go limp under pressure.

SPARKY. Ah, well, no, that's not much fun, is it? That happens sometimes. Eat lots of oysters, son. They'll help straighten out the pole.

(DORIS enters from the "kitchen" with a bowl of chicken soup and a roast beef sandwich which she brings to SPARKY in his chair.)

DORIS. I'm just fixing Sparky his evening meal, Larry. Soup 'n' San for $3.95. The house special.

SPARKY. Care to join us, son? Do we have enough, Mother?

DORIS. You got $3.95, son? Just joking. *(With a surprising edge.)* Of course we have enough, Sparky. Always have enough. Except when we don't and then you can have mine like you always do when there is only enough for one. *(Beat.)* Sorry. *(To LARRY.)* Did you let us know you were coming, son? If we'd known you were coming, I'd have baked a cake.

LARRY. I telephoned, but Dad said he was strangling someone and then you started giving me directions to where I was born.

DORIS. Oh, was that you? Thought you were the travel agent.

LARRY. Travel agent?

SPARKY. Maps and things for the great adventure, son. The big trip.

LARRY. The big trip? What trip?

SPARKY *(pointing to all the luggage stacked up by the front door)*. Yep, all packed 'n' ready to go! Camera, floss, toilet paper.

DORIS. Got to hit a home run before the game's over. That's what Sparky says.

SPARKY. Things to do, people to see!

DORIS. Don't talk drivel, Sparky. We don't see anyone. That's why we're taking this trip! Now eat your dinner. *(As SPARKY begins eating, DORIS pulls LARRY to one side.)*

It's been a while since you've been here, hasn't it? Things change, you know.

LARRY. Well, as I was saying to Dad, I've been working around the clock, Mom, but it seems—

DORIS. So busy you couldn't make it on our fortieth anniversary, could you!

LARRY. Mom, I was out of town on business, but I'm here now and I want to get closer to—

DORIS. Your father isn't the man he used to be, Larry. That's what I'm trying to say here. Time is taking its toll.

LARRY. He seems a little preoccupied, but his color's good and—

DORIS. I'm the glue that keeps us together, young man, day in and day out, and don't you forget it! More than a call now and then would be nice, you know. Grandparents need to see their grandchildren face to face once in a while. And you'd better find your focus quick 'cause without a compass your ass is grass! *(Beat.)* Sorry. Just got tired for a moment being supportive, available, dependable, and well-mannered. Won't happen again. *(DORIS exits into the "kitchen." SPARKY sips his soup while LARRY sits on one of his suitcases.)*

LARRY. I picked a bad time to come over, didn't I? Didn't really think you'd be doing anything.

SPARKY. Just getting older, eh?

LARRY. No, Dad, I didn't mean you and Mom don't have a life…it's just…I panicked and ran home. Damn, I never seem to know the right thing to do!

SPARKY *(not fully certain what his role is here)*. Isn't she a holy terror, though? Boy, oh boy. Forty-six years married to your mother. Don't know how I did it! Took a lot of Pepto Bismol. But I haven't been an easy assignment, either. It's a partnership, son.

LARRY. I've missed you. It's all going so fast! I look up from my desk and Kevin's starting to shave and I'm turning a little grey...and our...well...the marriage is...I think I'm dropping the ball, Dad. How do you and Mom do it?

SPARKY. Well, we don't do it anymore, son.

LARRY. I didn't mean—

SPARKY. Got one of those videos a year ago. Sex over Seventy? But I popped something in my back and then the pacemaker picked up a little tempo and—

LARRY. Pacemaker? What pacemaker? Did you tell me about a—

SPARKY *(in a confidential tone)*. Come here, son. Let me tell you something.

LARRY *(scoots his suitcase closer to SPARKY)*. Oh, thanks, Dad. I appreciate this.

SPARKY. You live together long enough, son, you run out of brilliant, original things to say.

LARRY. Yeah, I know. Sometimes we just sit in silence, don't even look at—

SPARKY. Then one day it just starts pouring out of you!

LARRY. What? What starts pouring out of you?

SPARKY. Ideas, son! Thoughts, images, insights! Wham! Bam! Just like that.

LARRY. Ideas? What ideas are those, Dad?

SPARKY. About the world around us! The formation of the cosmos, for example! That's a favorite of mine. How we got here. Where we're going. Are there enough seats left? These are crucial times, son.

LARRY. That's what I want to talk to you about, Dad. The future seems so—

SPARKY. But then!

LARRY. Yes? Then what?

SPARKY. But then your partner, your companion, the love of your life…ah…

LARRY. Michelle.

SPARKY. Michelle…two "ll's" or one?

LARRY. Two "ll's," Dad.

SPARKY *(giving the "thumbs-up" sign)*. Michelle with two "ll's" tells you that you've spouted these little gems before! Last month, or last week! Or while you were mowing the yard, or sitting on the john! Or having lunch at Denny's! Well, it can still be a great insight the second time around, can't it?

LARRY. Well, sure, you're just—

SPARKY. So you pull yourself together and puff out your chest and say *(Loudly.)* "Well, that's what I mean, woman! That's how I see the world. Now pass me the ketchup!"

DORIS *(from offstage)*. Don't you sass me, Sparky! Eat your soup.

LARRY *(laughing at the rapport between his parents)*. You two haven't changed a bit.

SPARKY. Well, she keeps me honest.

LARRY *(beat)*. It's great to be home. You look good, Dad.

SPARKY. Twenty sit-ups a day, a brisk walk around the block and plenty of prunes.

LARRY. Mom says maybe you're not—

SPARKY. The spark's still there, eh?

LARRY. Yes, sir, still there. You said you've had a pacemaker—

SPARKY. Still got the old get up and go, the old…

LARRY. Sparkle.

SPARKY. Sparkle!

LARRY & SPARKY *(playing out a routine they've played before)*. That's why they call me (you) Sparky!

SPARKY *(feeling as if he's done his fatherly duty).* Well, it's been a good visit, hasn't it? Covered the origin of my nickname and shared a little wisdom of the ages on how to keep a marriage fresh and alive. *(Looking at all the "stuff" LARRY has brought with him.)* After dinner I'll give you a hand with all this. The church has a garage sale next week. They'll be mighty happy you stopped by.

MICHELLE *(from offstage).* Larry! Larry!

LARRY. Dad, it's a bit more complicated than you think.

(MICHELLE enters. SPARKY is unaware of her presence.)

MICHELLE. Larry, tell him, please, and then let's get on with it.

SPARKY. Oh? There's more?

LARRY. It's about work. My job.

MICHELLE. Tell him we need the money, Larry.

LARRY. I've got some problems at work.

SPARKY. Problems?

MICHELLE. You said you'd ask him for—

SPARKY *(overlapping).* What kind of problems?

LARRY *(to MICHELLE).* I can't ask my father for—

MICHELLE. We can't make it on what I take home!

LARRY *(to MICHELLE).* It's not easy for me!

SPARKY. It's not supposed to be easy, son. It's supposed to be work. Pickin' 'em up and puttin' 'em down. Day after day.

MICHELLE *(overlapping).* It's the third notice, Larry!

SPARKY. They don't call it work because it's fun, son.

MICHELLE. They keep calling me at the office!

SPARKY *(continuing his train of thought).* They call it work because it's work. Thought you knew that.

LARRY *(to MICHELLE).* I know that! Get off my back!

SPARKY *(calling offstage)*. Mother! Hurry up with that grub. Larry's getting vicious.

LARRY *(overlapping)*. Dad, I'm sorry. I didn't mean—

SPARKY. I'll get out the old slides. I'll be right back. *(Calling offstage as he exits.)* I'm getting the slides, Mother. That should put us all to sleep.

DORIS *(from offstage)*. Don't start without me!

LARRY *(following after SPARKY)*. Dad, don't leave now. I didn't mean to—

(KEVIN enters with an earring in his ear and an "attitude.")

KEVIN. Dad! Hey, Pop? I need fifty bucks.

LARRY. Fifty bucks!

MICHELLE. Not now, Kevin! Please! Your father and I—

LARRY. What do you need fifty bucks for?

KEVIN. Hey, I got expenses.

LARRY. Expenses! You're sixteen years old! *(To MICHELLE.)* What expenses is he talking about?

MICHELLE. Larry, I can't keep it all together much longer. I have to work late at the office again tonight and—

LARRY. Work late at the office? What the hell's so important at the office? *(A car horn is heard offstage.)*

KEVIN. The guys are waiting for me, Pop, gimme some—

LARRY *(in frustration)*. Gimme some! Why does everybody want something from me? Please. You both said you'd give me a little time to sort things out and—

KEVIN *(overlapping)*. Ah, hell, I'm gonna move out! I'm bored outta my tree!

MICHELLE *(overlapping)*. Move out! What do you mean—

LARRY. You will not move out, Kevin! We're just going through some problems here.

KEVIN. I can work construction. Make good money. Won't have to beg anymore!

MICHELLE. You will not—

(SPARKY returns with a slide projector and a carousel.)

SPARKY. This should be fun, eh? A glimpse of the past. See how we've all aged.

LARRY. Dad, I don't think we need a memory walk here, OK? Maybe we can talk first and then—*(SPARKY has aimed the projector above the heads of the audience and now "turns on" the projector.)*

SPARKY. Eureka! It still works! Look at these slides, will ya! *(EVERYONE begins to get caught up in the family "slides." The actors should suggest the tone and content of the "slides" through body posture and facial animation. Ad libs could be utilized sparsely to punctuate their reactions. Possible "slides" might include a cookout, a family outing, LARRY in his Boy Scout or Little League uniform, SPARKY in his fishing gear, playing softball, DORIS looking strained in her role as helpmate, and so on.)*

KEVIN *(looking at the "slides")*. Hey, look at that. Is that you, Dad? Is that Grandma? Geez.

SPARKY. Your mother made that Halloween costume out of cardboard boxes, remember, Larry? You tripped carrying the jack-o'lantern and nearly went up in flames. But you didn't.

KEVIN. You were dorky looking, Dad.

SPARKY *(calling offstage)*. Mother! Come watch this. You're missing all the fun. *(SPARKY contributes chuckles relating to the "slides" but remains unaware of KEVIN and MICHELLE. More car horns are heard.)*

KEVIN. Hey, I gotta go. Can I have the fifty bucks?

MICHELLE *(to KEVIN)*. Are you going to tell your father about the windows, or do I have to—

LARRY. Windows? What windows?

KEVIN *(overlapping)*. Hey, a slight problem, that's all. No big deal.

MICHELLE *(overlapping)*. A slight problem? *(To LARRY.)* He and his friends broke some windows at school.

KEVIN. It was an accident.

MICHELLE. It was no accident! *(To LARRY.)* Have you seen his friends lately! They look—

KEVIN. Aw, geez! *(More car horns are heard offstage.)* Gimme a break here, will ya?

LARRY *(to KEVIN)*. How much damage?

KEVIN. Three hundred bucks.

LARRY. Three hundred bucks!

KEVIN *(fiercely)*. Just gimme the money, will ya? The guys are waiting!

MICHELLE. Then they can wait!

KEVIN *(as he begins to exit)*. Aw, forget it! I'll get it someplace else!

LARRY *(with MICHELLE's next line)*. Kevin, don't talk to me in that—

MICHELLE *(simultaneously)*. Don't you turn your back on—

KEVIN. Screw you both! *(Exits.)*

MICHELLE *(challenging LARRY)*. Where are you, Larry! Are you part of this family anymore? I can't do this alone, you hear me! *(Exits.)*

SPARKY *(laughing and pointing to the "screen")*. And there I am on the riding mower. Turned over. In the ditch.

LARRY. Dad, please, do we have to watch these now? I've got a problem with—

SPARKY. That's what family visits are for, son. Sit and look at the past. Thought you knew that. *(Calling offstage.)* Sweetheart!

(DORIS enters with chicken soup, a roast beef sandwich and a bowl of peanuts.)

DORIS. I knew you'd start without me. *(To LARRY.)* Isn't he awful? Married to your father six hundred years and I still can't get over how awful he is. But he's cute. A little puffy here and there, but cute all the same. Here, son. I'll fix your favorite chocolate cake in the morning when I get a breather. *(DORIS gives the meal to LARRY who sits on one of his suitcases. She then brings the bowl of nuts to SPARKY and sits on the arm of the chair to watch the "Slide Show.")* Aren't these fun, though? Look at that god-awful dress! What was I thinking of. There I am at the hospital fund raiser...and you at the Elks Club barbecue...I thought we were happier then.

SPARKY. Look at that fish, will you! Caught it all by myself.

DORIS *(confidentially to LARRY)*. Bought it at Safeway in the frozen food section. *(A "shot" of LARRY, DORIS and SPARKY.)*

SPARKY. Ah! Your college graduation.

DORIS. We were so proud of you, Larry. Your future ahead of you. Fixed you that big chocolate cake. Sparky, find the cake, sweetie.

LARRY. Dad, Mom. There's something I—*(A large chocolate birthday cake with "Go Get 'Em Larry" written on it comes on the "screen.")*

DORIS. Ah, there it is!

SPARKY. With "Go Get 'Em Larry" in big white letters. There they are. See? Melting off to the side, see?

DORIS. Then you took off and we didn't see you for years.

SPARKY. Gotta get 'em while you can, Mother. Isn't that right, son?

LARRY. I can't get 'em anymore, Dad. That's what I've been trying to tell you. They keep slipping through my fingers.

SPARKY. We know what you mean, son.

DORIS. That's why we're going now.

LARRY. Going where now, Mom?

SPARKY. We looked at ourselves in the mirror the other day, son. It was scary.

DORIS. We just stood there and screamed.

SPARKY. They were getting away from us, son.

DORIS. The days. The months. The years!

SPARKY. And we knew it was time.

DORIS. Bangkok. Singapore!

SPARKY. The hanging gardens of Babylon.

DORIS. Venice, Rome.

SPARKY. Cleveland. *(Pantomimes being Elvis with a guitar.)*

LARRY. How far?

DORIS. Around the world, if I can last.

LARRY. Around the world! You can't!

DORIS. Yes, we can.

LARRY. Not now!

SPARKY. It's now or never, Larry.

LARRY. When?

DORIS. The day after tomorrow.

LARRY. The day after tomorrow!

DORIS. Sparky's prostate has fallen asleep for the time being—

SPARKY. And Mother's heart is still pumping so—

LARRY *(the pressure finally explodes as he blurts it all out)*. You can't! Not yet. Please! I need me some time! I need you. I've lost my job. Michelle's working overtime every night. The savings account is empty. The house needs a new roof. My car's got 100,000 miles on it! I can't talk to my son! I don't know who I am anymore! I want to make it work like it's supposed to but I don't think I can keep it up! *(There is a considerable pause.)*

DORIS. Oh, dear. Son. What's happened, Larry?

SPARKY. Lost your job? Shouldn't lose your job, son.

LARRY. I know, Dad. I know.

SPARKY. Better get it back.

LARRY. It was the numbers.

DORIS. Numbers? What numbers?

LARRY. They weren't high enough. I couldn't...I don't seem to have the—

(LARRY's BOSS appears in a pool of light.)

THE BOSS. ...old productivity you used to have, Larry? The old get up and go?

LARRY *(to his BOSS)*. Yes, sir. And I feel badly about that. But I'm sure I'll get the old get up an go up again, sir. It's just a temporary setback. Can't seem to keep—

THE BOSS. We've been fair with you, Larry, haven't we?

LARRY. Absolutely, sir, and—

THE BOSS. Paid you well?

LARRY. Fairly well, yes, sir, but...sir? Paid me well? You're not going to pay me anymore? You mean I'm—

THE BOSS. Benefits. Free coffee. Bathroom facilities. Cool air in the summer. Warm air in the winter. It's not a bad trade off. But you pulled the plug.

LARRY. It's the work! It keeps coming!

THE BOSS. You shouldn't have pulled the plug, Larry.

LARRY. E-mail, memos, faxes, meetings, responsibilities, power lunches! There's too much work! I just couldn't breathe. I had to breathe!

THE BOSS. Breathe on your own time, Larry.

LARRY. It was a protest of sorts, sir.

THE BOSS. These aren't the sixties, Larry.

DORIS *(responding to the presence of THE BOSS)*. Who is this obnoxious man?

LARRY. This is my boss, Mom, Dad.

THE BOSS *(with a general acknowledgment)*. Folks.

DORIS *(reluctantly, but always the hostess)*. Care for some soup? I have some soup left.

LARRY. Mom! Please!

THE BOSS. Everything OK at home, Larry? How is Maggie?

LARRY. Michelle.

SPARKY *(to THE BOSS)*. Two "ll's."

THE BOSS *(giving SPARKY a "thumbs-up" acknowledgment)*. Thank you, sir. *(To LARRY.)* We don't want everything not OK at home, do we, Larry? Cuts down on the numbers. We need happy campers all around.

LARRY. That's part of the problem, sir. Michelle and I don't see each other very much, and Kevin is getting in with a bad crowd and uh…I…uh…I'm behind the plow from dawn to…I do good work but it's not getting any easier! I need an assistant.

THE BOSS. No can do, Larry.

DORIS *(to THE BOSS)*. Larry wouldn't ask for an assistant if he didn't need one!

THE BOSS. Larry's a big boy, Mother. He knows the numbers.

LARRY. Sir, I take work home every night. Work every weekend.

SPARKY. Way to go, son!

THE BOSS. But you pulled the plug.

DORIS. What did you do, Larry?

LARRY. It was annual report time and I was working late. Statistics…vectors…factors. All coming in at me on the screen…wave after wave…and I just felt like pulling the plug…so I did! And it all crashed. Graphs and charts and columns! All gone! The entire system. Everything. Then I went to the back-up and pulled the plug on it, too. I pressed "delete" for three hours. All the numbers just vanished like magic. It felt wonderful! And then the screen went black. *(Beat.)* It was so quiet.

DORIS. Oh, dear.

THE BOSS. See what I mean, folks?

LARRY. I was getting these anxiety attacks. The doctor says it's stress.

THE BOSS *(no longer interested in being sociable).* Of course it's stress. What else is there? No pain, no gain! It's a big world out there! Alaska, Africa, Cleveland. Wake up and smell the espresso, Larry. You screwed the pooch.

DORIS *(to THE BOSS).* His heart could use a rest, that's all.

THE BOSS. Big business isn't about heart, Mother. Get a hearing aid! It's about numbers. No numbers, no job. Everybody knows that. *(Noticing the slide with everybody celebrating around the chocolate cake.)* Hey, great looking cake. What's that dribbling off the side there? "Go Get 'Em Larry." Yeah, well, you shoulda thought of that before you pulled the plug, Larry. *(Nodding to DORIS and SPARKY.)* Folks. *(THE BOSS exits.)*

DORIS. What an asshole.

SPARKY. You're up a creek, son.

LARRY. I know, Dad.

DORIS. What can we do, Larry? How can we help?

LARRY. Let me stay here and bunk in with the two of you for a while. You, Dad and the Great Books. I need to find some direction again. Everyone depends on me and I'm dropping the ball. Michelle, Kevin, the job. I pulled the plug. That's not a sign of good health. Can't escape from life, I know that. So I've got to find the answers. And they're here. I know they are.

DORIS *(as she and SPARKY exchange looks)*. Son, we're going to be as direct as we can.

LARRY. Fine, yes. Oh, please, that's what I want.

DORIS. We love you. Very much.

SPARKY. You know we do.

LARRY. I know that, Mom. Dad.

DORIS. But we've got to take this trip. Now.

SPARKY. Not next year.

DORIS. Not next month. Tomorrow. There are things you do now, son.

SPARKY. You learn that as you mature.

DORIS. You're getting older, Larry, but are you maturing?

LARRY. Yes, I am. That's why I've come—

DORIS. So whatever you're here to learn, son, get on the stick.

SPARKY *(referring to LARRY's books)*. You've got a lot of heavy reading here.

DORIS. We think that's wonderful.

SPARKY. But we won't be here to read them with you, son.

DORIS. We'll be in Istanbul or Mozambique, wherever that is!

SPARKY. We have one doctor's visit left, then we're off.

DORIS. You want to get close, son? That's wonderful. Last year would have been a good time. Even after we come back. Come visit then. But tomorrow we're off to see the world.

SPARKY *(singing à la* The Wizard of Oz*).* The wonderful world of—

DORIS. Sparky!! Keep it focused! *(Beat.)* Do you see what I mean, Larry? You think time's your ally, then it turns on you. You've got to know when it's going to turn.

LARRY *(beat).* You're right. I'm sorry. This is all wrong. It's selfish of me. I show up out of the blue, expect you to rearrange your life. *(LARRY moves to his gear.)* I'll get a hotel room tonight and tomorrow morning I'll—

SPARKY. Not on your life. You'll spend the night with us.

DORIS *(beginning to exit).* I'll get your pillow. Then we'll have a talk, take our medicine, lock the doors, turn out the lights and see if we all wake up alive in the morning. *(DORIS exits.)*

SPARKY. I don't know what to say, son. I'm sorry. It's bad timing. Bad things always happen at the wrong time. That's why they're bad.

LARRY. I just began to crack. Everything just fell in on me like an avalanche.

SPARKY. It's mortality, son. Happens to all of us sooner or later.

LARRY. Mortality?

SPARKY. Yep. It comes knocking on the door. Do you hear it? It's time.

LARRY. Time? Time for what?

SPARKY. Just time, son. That's what we're talking about here. You'll hear it when it starts coming after you. Everyone does eventually. Clump, Clump, clump. Like that T-Rex in *Jurassic Park.* But you've got to stand up and stare it right in the face before you cash it all in, right, Mother?

(DORIS enters with a pillow and pillowcase.)

DORIS. Sometimes I want to cash it all in and run off with the grocery boy.

SPARKY. She's dreaming, son. Grocery boy wouldn't have her.

DORIS. Big blonde kid with muscles out to here. Lifts those sacks…the sweat beads up on his neck…makes me want to lean over and—

SPARKY. Mother! We're joshing around, son, that's all. Do you and the Missus joke around now and then? It's real important, isn't it, Mother?

DORIS. Nothing but Mardi Gras around here, Larry. A three-ring circus. *(Calling offstage.)* Could we have the bedroom on now, please? We're on a tight schedule here!

(A PROPS ASSISTANT moves on a simple bed covered by a young boy's bedspread. Various items are cluttered on top of it. DORIS says "Thank you" and begins clearing items off the bed and fixing the pillow.)

DORIS. I'll just move these over here.

SPARKY. And I'll get your pajamas, son. Then we'll tuck you in like the good old days. *(SPARKY begins opening one of LARRY's suitcases in search of LARRY's pajamas.)*

LARRY. Dad, I can do that. I'm a little too old for a tuck-in. What I need is some—

DORIS. One good night's sleep at your mother's and you'll be your old self again.

LARRY. Mom, I don't think you and Dad understand. Life's scaring the hell out of me!

DORIS. What do you think it's doing to the rest of us? That's how it should be, son. Keeps you on your toes.

SPARKY *(having discovered some of LARRY's Great Books)*. Do you have *Ivanhoe* in here somewhere? Now, that's a great book. *Far from the Madding Crowd.* That's good advice. Stay as far away as you can. *Treasure Island,* Mother. No man's an island, son, treasure or no treasure. I can vouch for that. *Critique of Pure Reason.* Now there's a page turner! Whoa, what's this! *The Way of All Flesh.* Could I borrow this one for the evening? Ah, *The Three Musketeers*! *(Assuming a "fencing" stance.)* All for one, and one for all! Charge!! *(SPARKY "fences" his way across the "living room" and beckons LARRY to join in. The two MEN "fence" until SPARKY gets "hit.")* Fair Rosalyn...don't leave me! I'm dying! Ah, sweet sorrow...Juliet is such a nice person...I shall miss you! *(SPARKY "dies" with melodramatic flair.)*

DORIS *(applauding).* Bravo, Sparky. One of my all-time favorites. *(To LARRY.)* Your father "dies" periodically. Watches "The Days of Our Lives"...dies, the "Disease of the Week" movie...dies. I come in sometimes and he's draped over the chair. One Sunday we were out driving and Sparky just let out a groan.

SPARKY. Flapped my arms in the air.

DORIS. "Sparky! Not now," I said. "You can't die now." I had to grab the wheel.

SPARKY. She pulled me back from the brink, son. That's what a good woman will do. But not forever. Clump, clump, clump.

DORIS *(to LARRY).* He'll be done in just a minute. Gets a little crazy without his medicine.

LARRY. What medicine is that, Mom?

DORIS. For when you get old, son. Old people take medicine. It's the law. You'll see. Sparky, behave yourself while I'm gone! *(DORIS exits.)*

LARRY. Dad, what the hell is going on? Are you all right?

SPARKY *(changing his tone dramatically).* Is she gone, son? Take a look. We don't have much time before she gets back.

LARRY *(perplexed, looks offstage).* Uh, yeah, I think she's—

SPARKY *(moves quickly to LARRY).* I'm worried about your mother. She's not well. She keeps talking about taking long trips.

LARRY. But you just said it was now or never, didn't you?

SPARKY. It's for her sake, son. I play along. It's just for laughs. Pulling me back from the brink and all. All this dying business takes the bite out of it...you remember that poem...Death, put away your stinger! You see?

LARRY. But what about your pacemaker, and your medicine?

SPARKY. You don't know what it's like with your mother. "Home Shopping Network" and "QVC" damn near twenty-four hours a day. I'd come home from a haircut and we'd have a new television set!

(The PROPS ASSISTANT enters with an impressive television set and places it in front of the wing-back chair. The ASSISTANT exits and will bring on most if not all of what SPARKY mentions.)

SPARKY. Those 25th Anniversary Commemorative Elvis plates? You know the ones I mean? She ordered a dozen. The Music of the Month Club? Signed up for fifty years. Every day I play a new one, son, but I can't keep up. We're going to get symphonies by composers who haven't even been born yet. And a new vacuum cleaner...we already have three!...fake leather-bound copies of the *Complete Works of Agatha Christie*...something to read on the trip, she says...a dozen baseballs autographed by Larry Bird...how did that happen!...and a pair of snowshoes!

(When the PROPS ASSISTANT is finished, SPARKY fumbles for a tip.) Uh, son, do you have any change on you? *(LARRY comes to SPARKY's rescue. The PROPS ASSISTANT says "Thanks" and exits.)*

LARRY. Snowshoes? What is Mom going to do with all this, Dad?

SPARKY. It's like the Pharaohs, son. Just like the Pharaohs.

LARRY. The Pharaohs?

SPARKY. Making preparations.

LARRY. Preparations for what, Dad?

SPARKY. The trip, son.

LARRY. I don't understand.

SPARKY. It's all part of the plan.

LARRY. Plan? What plan is that, Dad? I'm getting left behind here.

(The TRAVEL AGENT arrives amid SOUNDS of cruise ship whistles and airport arrival and departure announcements for Morocco, Buenos Aires, Istanbul, etc. These "voice-over" SOUND BITES should be in a series of foreign languages—Russian, Norwegian, French, and so on. The AGENT might wheel on a display board featuring a variety of promotional photos: close-ups of people enjoying an elegant dinner on a cruise ship, frolicking with green parrots, greedily hanging over roulette tables, waving out of sleek tour buses, wearing outrageous floral shirts.)

TRAVEL AGENT. Hello, hello, hello! Bon voyage, one and all! Sparky, sweetheart, you look divine.

SPARKY *(responding to the posters)*. Look, son! Norway, Turkey, Singapore! It's all here. Isn't this something, though! *(Calling offstage.)* Doris! Come quick. The world has just arrived.

TRAVEL AGENT *(noticing LARRY)*. Hello there! You're cute. Are you going along for the ride? You're a little young for this batch, but I can wedge you in somewhere.

LARRY. No, thanks, I don't think I'll be going on...what the hell is all—

(DORIS enters with SPARKY's medicine.)

TRAVEL AGENT. Ah, there she is! I love your hair.

DORIS *(to the AGENT)*. You're late.

TRAVEL AGENT. Oh, I know. I'm so sorry.

DORIS. Any problems?

TRAVEL AGENT. Everything's all set!

DORIS. Good. Want any chicken soup?

TRAVEL AGENT. I've eaten, thank you.

DORIS. So you don't want my chicken soup? Fine. Sparky, take your medicine.

SPARKY *(while taking several spoonfuls of his medicine. Getting wound up about the journey)*. The Tower of London, son! The Colossus of Rhodes, Club Med! Naked bodies everywhere!

DORIS *(to the AGENT)*. Get on with it. Sparky's fading. We don't have a lifetime here.

TRAVEL AGENT. You do at Universal Travel, Doris. You have an eternity. *(We hear a loud drum roll and crashing cymbal.)*

DORIS *(with a sense of unease)*. Sparky? Where did that come from!

TRAVEL AGENT. At Universal Travel your every wish is our command. Four-star hotels every night!.

DORIS. Sleep 'til noon?

TRAVEL AGENT. Sleep forever. And delicious gourmet dishes you can't pronounce!

SPARKY. No more chicken soup.

TRAVEL AGENT *(picking up the tempo)*. Entrance fees to museums with long corridors and no bathrooms, seats at the world's most boring operas, coupon booklets to the sex shops of Shanghai!

DORIS. Sparky!

SPARKY *(with enthusiasm)*. We can take the elevator to the top of the Eiffel Tower, Mother.

TRAVEL AGENT. To the top of St. Peter's, if you want, Sparky!

LARRY *(to the AGENT)*. I don't think they have an elevator to the top of—

TRAVEL AGENT. Stay out of this! My commission's astronomical! *(Putting on the "bite.")* The Caribbean! Santiago, Moscow, Stockholm, Cincinnati—

SPARKY. Cleveland!

TRAVEL AGENT. Cleveland! All transfers and taxes included. And souvenir memories captured on faded Polaroid snapshots taken by Claus, Achmed, Gundle, Ling Su and Ramon! A trip you'll never forget for the rest of your very short life. *(The AGENT produces an ornate scroll.)* All I need is your final signature and the universe is yours.

DORIS *(suddenly quite concerned)*. Oh, Sparky, is this what we really want to do? Are we doing the right thing?

SPARKY. Don't you want to go?

DORIS. Do you? You do, don't you? I want you to be happy.

SPARKY. If you do, sweetheart, I do. Of course you do, don't you? I do, I think.

DORIS. Sometimes I just want to curl up into a little ball and roll away.

TRAVEL AGENT. Can't do that, Doris. We're all connected. One big family of Man. Time to meet the family!

LARRY. Dad, how about just two weeks in Cancun, maybe?

TRAVEL AGENT *(to LARRY)*. Hey, buzz off!

DORIS. Larry's right. Maybe we should slow down and just visit with him and Michelle and—

TRAVEL AGENT. Let Larry solve his own problems, Doris. If you and Sparky here move any slower, your blood'll stop flowing!

SPARKY. We don't want that, do we, Doris?

LARRY. You can't talk to my parents that—

TRAVEL AGENT *(intensifying the pitch)*. The Gold Coast, the Silver Coast, the Bronze Coast! I don't give a damn, whatever the hell you want...It's now or never! *(With a flourish to the heavens.)* Hit it! *(Suddenly the lights flicker and we hear a massive thunder clap.)*

SPARKY. Eureka! *(Swept up in the fervor of the moment, SPARKY takes the pen and signs the "contract.")*

LARRY. Dad?

DORIS. Sparky, what have we done!

TRAVEL AGENT. That was close. *(To LARRY.)* You almost screwed the pooch again. OK, folks, you sail at midnight tomorrow! No turning back now! The universe is yours! *(The AGENT tosses confetti into the air and exits.)* Was that a sales pitch or what!

DORIS. Midnight! Well. There you are then, I guess we're off to see the universe whether we want to or not. It all seems so sudden.

SPARKY *(with great buoyancy)*. Tell you what. My treat. How about some milk and cookies before bed to celebrate the great adventure? That'll put us right as rain. Clear as day. Dark as night. And so on! Now, where is that kitchen? *(SPARKY exits to the "kitchen.")*

LARRY. Is Dad all right, Mom? He seems a little...

DORIS. Spacey? You're right there.

LARRY. He's doing this for you, Mom. He loves you.

DORIS. Of course he loves me! I'm lovable. But what does that have to do with it? *(DORIS moves to the bed and sits. LARRY joins her.)* You don't know what it's been like! He wants to take these trips. Brochures, specials, bonanzas! In the mailbox every day! "We have to go before the final curtain," he says. And this trip on top of the hospital bills—

LARRY. Hospital bills! I didn't know about—

DORIS. You don't call. You don't write. You think you're the only one in this world? Well, we're still here, Larry, right along with "Home Shopping" and "QVC" and it's too much! He picks up the telephone and he's off to the races. I come home from the grocery store and we have a new television set!

(The PROPS ASSISTANT enters with another television set. DORIS waves the PROPS ASSISTANT away.)

DORIS. Oh, that's all right. It's all out here already. I think Larry's got the picture. *(The PROPS ASSISTANT exits looking a bit put out.)* What am I going to do with three vacuums? I can't get him to pick up his socks. He says it gives him a sense of power to accumulate things.

LARRY. Preparations for the big journey. Like the Pharaohs.

DORIS. You got it.

LARRY. So, all this isn't yours?

DORIS. It is now, isn't it! I love your father dearly, son, but some of his elevators are stuck.

(SPARKY enters with a tray of gingersnaps and three glasses of milk. He joins LARRY and DORIS on the bed.)

SPARKY. Here we are. Gingersnaps and some nice cold milk.

LARRY. Thanks, Dad.

DORIS. Isn't this a lovely family picture, though. Well, a lovely, partial family picture. Let's take a nice, long, swig of milk, shall we? Like we used to in the good old days. *(All three drink in unison.)*

SPARKY. Ah, whole milk with all the fat left in it. Like we used to like it.

DORIS. "Good for you!" they used to say in the good old days.

SPARKY. But then they stopped saying "Good for you!"

DORIS. And started scaring us to death with cholesterol and fatty fats, and then came Stairmaster and Nordic Flex. *(Beat.)* My, but that young man has a body to die for.

SPARKY. Mother...

LARRY. Mom?

DORIS. The way his sweat glistens in that golden light makes me—

SPARKY. It's time for the news, Doris. A little news, a little weather, then a little shut-eye. *(To LARRY.)* See what I mean? Your mother's on the edge.

DORIS. Sorry. Lost my focus for a moment. But I'm back...I think I'm back...why do I want to come back?

LARRY. My God! I had no idea. It just happens, doesn't it? I've lost track of you. It's all slipping away from me!

DORIS. You think it's slipping now! Wait until you reach our age.

(The TV ANNOUNCER appears in a spotlight.)

TV ANNOUNCER. Good evening, ladies and gentlemen and welcome to the *News of Your World.*

DORIS. Brace yourselves everyone.

TV ANNOUNCER. The top story tonight focuses on the increasingly common behavior of ordinary, plodding but well-meaning individuals, to collapse under the increasing pressures of daily existence.

(As the TV ANNOUNCER continues, MICHELLE enters, disheveled, with a whisky glass in her hand. As this segment progresses EVERYONE will eventually acknowledge each other's presence.)

MICHELLE. I couldn't help it, Larry. It just happened.

TV ANNOUNCER. At 4:55 this afternoon in the Sunshine Grocery Mart on South Clemson…

MICHELLE. I couldn't reach you at the office and Kevin didn't come home from school.

TV ANNOUNCER. …an attractive woman entering the first stages of early middle-age began her weekly shopping. After carefully stacking two hundred and twenty-three cans of Diet Pepsi in her shopping cart, she suddenly broke into tears.

MICHELLE. The committee rejected my proposal, Larry, and the vice principal said Kevin hadn't been in school for three days! Where does he go, Larry? I'm doing my best, Larry, but I'm failing. I felt all alone!

DORIS *(talking directly to MICHELLE while the others still "watch" MICHELLE on television)*. And all you could do was cry, I know, you poor thing.

MICHELLE *(to DORIS)*. Yes.

DORIS. And you felt this pressure building up!

MICHELLE. Yes. It was seizing me here.

TV ANNOUNCER. She claimed to be suffocating—

MICHELLE *(angrily to the ANNOUNCER)*. I was suffocating!

DORIS *(clutches her chest)*. Here? Right here!

MICHELLE. Yes. I couldn't breathe.

DORIS. And then suddenly...*(In unison, MICHELLE and DORIS release their anxiety in one, long, extended scream. LARRY and SPARKY react to the screaming.)*

LARRY *(to MICHELLE)*. Michelle, are you—

SPARKY *(overlapping to DORIS)*. Sweetheart, are you all—

TV ANNOUNCER. The screams set off a chain reaction. In less than a minute, thirty-nine women and sixteen men combined to create what is now believed to be the biggest primal scream in grocery store history.

MICHELLE. The manager was very nice, Larry. He let me sit in his office. Gave me a bottle of Evian. Wasn't that nice of him? I couldn't make another decision, Larry! Meetings, memos, Kevin, casseroles, exercise classes, Kevin, watering the plants, doing the laundry! I'm on the Business Women's Committee for a Better Tomorrow and I can't even make it through today. Where am I in all this, Larry? Who am I? I feel so trivial sometimes and I'm not! I just started screaming.

DORIS. I know. Sometimes I just can't keep it in either.

MICHELLE. I couldn't see a way out, where to go. What purpose to make out of my life!

LARRY. Michelle, I'm trying to get a grip on—

MICHELLE. It's not always about you. It's about us! You're so self-centered.

DORIS. Way to go, dear.

MICHELLE. I have a...friend at the office, Larry.

LARRY. A friend? What do you mean a friend?

MICHELLE. You have a friend, don't you, Larry?

LARRY. Oh, Michelle, no. It's not...she doesn't mean anything to me...I don't know why I—

MICHELLE. It's been building for months. He listens to me.

LARRY. I listen to you! I'm right here. See, I'm listening now!

MICHELLE. He hasn't touched me yet, Larry. But I think I want him to.

TV ANNOUNCER. Well, this is getting juicy. I love this job.

LARRY *(to ANNOUNCER)*. Why don't you shut up!

DORIS. Larry, that's not the way to keep a marriage going. It'll tear your heart out.

SPARKY. You should be tending your own garden, son.

LARRY. I don't have time for a garden, Dad. I'm out there slaying dragons! Isn't that what we're supposed to do? *(To MICHELLE.)* I don't know who I am either but if I stop to find out the next guy's right behind me to take my place. I don't think I can keep up!

(KEVIN speaks from offstage and then enters.)

KEVIN. Dad, where you been? Dad? I got suspended. Thirty-two days of detention. Cool, huh? It's a school record.

LARRY. Suspended! Ah, Kevin, no!

SPARKY *(to KEVIN)*. That's nothing to be proud of, young man. Who are these slime ball friends you hang out with?

KEVIN. They aren't slime balls, Granddad, they're just—

DORIS. Not now. Tell your grandfather about it in the morning.

SPARKY. We'll go fishing.

KEVIN. Fishing! Aw, man, the gang's all going up to the—

MICHELLE. Kevin, behave!

KEVIN. I hate fishing! Dad, do I have to—

SPARKY. You and I and your dad.

LARRY. Oh, boy.

DORIS. That's what families do. A little fishing. Some dry sandwiches. Maybe a little chocolate cake if I can get around to it. *(Taking the whisky glass from MICHELLE.)* And tomorrow you and I will have some hot tea and toss around all the guilt we can stand.

MICHELLE. I'd like that very much, thank you.

SPARKY *(feeling empowered as head of the family)*. OK, let's let it all hang out. The Great Books my ass! Life's not a library, son. Life's about living. Good times and bad times. It's all a banquet but sometimes you've got to scrub hard in the kitchen.

TV ANNOUNCER *(chuckling)*. Scrub hard in the kitchen! Where did you come up with—

SPARKY *(to ANNOUNCER)*. Stay out of this! *(To LARRY.)* We're older, son, and some of the gears don't make contact like they used to.

DORIS. But we don't miss much, Larry.

SPARKY. Now, we don't exactly know what it is we know all the time we know it. If we knew that, it'd be a lot to remember.

DORIS. And time's moving on, Larry. So are you going to 'fess up so we can all get on with our lives—

SPARKY. Or are we going to have to start kicking some butt? *(Lightning and a loud clap of thunder. The LIGHTS flicker.)*

TV ANNOUNCER. Lightning struck an American household tonight when members of a dysfunctional family considered the prospects of facing each other as human beings. Update at 11:00. *(EVERYONE slowly turns to the AUDIENCE with a "deer caught in the headlights" look on their faces.)*

BLACKOUT—END OF ACT ONE

ACT TWO

AT RISE: *LIGHTS reveal Larry's bedroom where we discover LARRY sitting on his bed reading several of his Great Books. By the look of things, he has been reading a great deal. KEVIN enters with a glass of milk and some gingersnaps, and watches his father for a moment.*

KEVIN. Hi.

LARRY. Oh, hi. Everything OK?

KEVIN. Yeah. Fine. I got some gingersnaps from the kitchen. And some milk. Think that's OK?

LARRY. Sure.

KEVIN *(moving into the bedroom)*. So, this is your old room. Hard to think of you as a kid once.

LARRY. Me, too. Seems centuries ago.

KEVIN. Pick your nose and read dirty books?

LARRY. Guess I did. You do that?

KEVIN. You bet. Got to. *(Beat.)* Watcha doin'?

LARRY. Trying to read these books.

KEVIN. Are they dirty?

LARRY. Not very. They're supposed to be great. All the wisdom of the ages. Did you know...*(Skimming and paraphrasing from Spengler's* The Decline of the West.*)*...that servitude and freedom...is...how we distinguish vegetable from animal existence...(but) "only the plant is wholly and entirely what it is"?

KEVIN. What else would it be?

LARRY *(continues paraphrasing the material).* But that "an animal is a vegetable (and) something more besides. A herd that huddles together trembling in the presence of danger," in other words, we can sense a threat to our safety, or "a child that clings weeping to its mother..." Is that what I'm doing here?

KEVIN. Doesn't sound healthy to me.

LARRY *(pressing on).* "All of these animals, including us, are seeking to give up the responsibilities of freedom" of choice and consequences, I think he means, and "return to the vegetal servitude from which they originally came." I guess that's me.

KEVIN. Spengler's *The Decline of the West.*

LARRY. Yeah, how did you know?

KEVIN. It's on the front of the cover.

LARRY *(chuckling).* You never stop, do you?

KEVIN. He says that when we realized we were no longer the center of the universe, that the universe was a chaotic presence of unpredictability and harm...we got frightened and...uh...lots of stuff began to happen.

LARRY. Bad stuff, I bet.

KEVIN. Yeah, bad stuff.

LARRY. You've read Spengler?

KEVIN. Na. I saw the movie.

LARRY *(having fun).* I don't think they made a movie about—

KEVIN. Yeah, they did. Kevin Costner, Johnny Depp...

LARRY. And Madonna, I bet.

KEVIN. So, you saw it, too, huh? *(Beat.)* Read it in detention hall.

LARRY. Oh.

KEVIN. So, you got O.J.'s book here?

LARRY. Kevin.

KEVIN. Hey, either you got the great books or you don't. *(KEVIN picks up a few books.) The Prince and the Pauper.* That reminds me. What about my allowance? Just joking. Hey, *Moby Dick*! Story about a guy who has a thing for this whale, right?

LARRY. When I was a kid, Granddad used to read passages of it before we went fishing. Said it gave him special powers.

KEVIN. Did they yell at you?

LARRY. Who?

KEVIN. Grandma, Granddad. When you were a kid. You know.

LARRY. Yell?

KEVIN. Yeah, shout. Yell. The way we do all the time.

LARRY. Do you and I yell all the time?

KEVIN. Seems like it sometimes.

LARRY *(beat)*. I don't remember but I guess they did. They must have. They're parents. It's not easy, Kevin. It's always a battle of wills. Mine against theirs.

KEVIN. Yours against mine?

LARRY. Yep.

KEVIN. Who's winning? *(LARRY eyes KEVIN a moment.)* So, is it working out? Coming back here?

LARRY. I don't know. Everything looks foreign to me. Can't remember this room. What I used to do or what I played with. What my dreams were. I've lost track of everything! Dad has a pacemaker I didn't know about. "Didn't want to bother you, son. You're always so busy!" My mother looks exhausted. I've lost track of my life...your life...your mother's life.

KEVIN. You're not supposed to do that. You're the dad.

LARRY. I know, Kevin. I'm getting there, though.

KEVIN. Can I leave, too?

LARRY. Leave? Leave where?

KEVIN. With Stevie. We can detail cars and make a ton of money and be out of your hair forever. Maybe pick up a third roommate, help out with expenses. Thought we'd all chip in and give it a shot. What do ya say?

LARRY. No. You can't leave. Not yet.

KEVIN. You did.

LARRY. We have to get to know each other better first.

KEVIN. But you left. And all Mom does at night, late sometimes, is walk back and forth in the kitchen. Crying. Banging pots around. Gets real noisy.

LARRY. But I'm coming back.

KEVIN. Mom doesn't think so.

LARRY. We're a family, and families stay together. They fall apart sometimes but—

KEVIN. Hey, when you gotta go, you gotta go!

LARRY. It's too soon for you to go. Stay and help your mother. Please. I'm making all the mistakes one family can take right now, OK?

KEVIN. I don't help her out now and she's OK.

LARRY. She doesn't sound OK to me.

KEVIN. Well, don't take all day to find your focus, 'cause I got a life, too.

LARRY. Hey, the bottom just fell out. The pressures. I got blindsided.

KEVIN. You think adults are the only ones feeling any pressure?

LARRY. No, I didn't mean that. It's just that it's hard to do everything right all the time and —

KEVIN. All we do is slip on our Reeboks and dance down the halls, right?

LARRY. Of course not. You don't know where you're going when you're a kid, I was just like that, I understand, and then there's pressure for grades and then new rules keep comin' at you, it's just one thing after...tell me about the suspension at school.

KEVIN. Aw, not now, will ya, Dad!

LARRY. Did one of the guy's dare you to—

KEVIN. Stuff happens, OK?

LARRY. Aw, come on. Don't be like that. Let's talk about it.

KEVIN. Can I have the car keys?

LARRY. Now?

KEVIN. Yes, now.

LARRY. You just came in.

KEVIN. Well, I want to go back out!

LARRY. Where?

KEVIN. Out. Here. There. Anywhere.

LARRY. No. Not tonight. Stay in and we can talk a bit.

KEVIN. Come on, Dad, just gimme—

LARRY. No. Stay here a while, OK and—

KEVIN. I'll just sit here and listen to you solve all my problems, and I don't think you've got the qualifications!

LARRY *(beat)*. What do I get in return?

KEVIN. Aw, come on!

LARRY. I give you the keys and you give me what in return? It's fair.

KEVIN. What can I give you in return, Dad? I don't have anything! You have it all. Just gimme the keys so I can get outta here and breathe on my own! Then I'll come back to prison, OK? Double lock the front door, flip off the light you left on for me, and count my blessings my Dad cares enough to ask about my friends and my schooling and who I talk to and what I think about and what I spend the money on that he gives me each week so I can learn how to budget my life!

LARRY. I just want to make sure you can make it when you—

KEVIN. Grow up? Like you did? Oh, yeah. I forgot those weekly visits with the shrink who asks what I feel about my dad pulling the plug at work and running back to his parents—

LARRY. I'm not running back, I'm just—

KEVIN. And my mom losing it in the grocery store. My friends got a big kick outta seeing that on TV. *(Beat.)* Hey, this has been a great father-son moment, hasn't it? *(Exits.)*

LARRY. Kevin, I'm sorry for...come back, I want to talk!

(LORAINE enters dressed in slip and hose. She will finish dressing as the scene progresses. She is holding a towel in her hands.)

LORAINE. We don't have time to talk, Larry. I don't want to be caught in traffic. *(LORAINE finishes toweling herself.)* Every time we stay at the Carlton, I say to myself, "Take this towel home, Loraine, and hang it up in the bathroom and see how long it takes Roger to notice it." "Who's Carlton, Loraine?" he'd ask. And I'd say "It's the hotel where Larry and I meet to rendezvous each Wednesday afternoon, dear, and whoops, you cut your cheek." I wonder what he'd say next.

LARRY. Something memorable, I'm sure.

LORAINE. Do you want to leave first or shall—

LARRY *(smiling weakly)*. I'm sorry about...

LORAINE. That's all right. You've been tired lately.

LARRY. I've had a lot on my mind. Been reading a lot.

LORAINE. It's not a problem. I love us every time. You know that. Even if you don't...it's not a problem.

LARRY. I do, too, yes, I always love us every time, but today I...

LORAINE. Sshh. That's all right.

LARRY. Do you really?

LORAINE. Do I what really?

LARRY. Love us every time? It. Us.

LORAINE. Yes, of course I do. I just said I did, didn't I?

LARRY. Yes.

LORAINE. You believe me, don't you? That I love it every time? Regardless.

LARRY. Yes, of course, but...

LORAINE. What do you mean "Yes, of course, but..."? I said I did, didn't I? Every time. Wonderful. Sparkling. Takes me to another level. Except today. Which was wonderful, too. In its special way.

LARRY. I just want to talk about us for a moment, and...us, that's all.

LORAINE. Darling, I want to talk about everything you want to talk about but time is—

LARRY. I don't want to be wrong!

LORAINE. Wrong! Wrong about what?

LARRY. About us.

LORAINE. Wrong? In what way wrong?

LARRY. I mean, we agreed that we'd just settle our anxieties...well...enjoy each other.

LORAINE. Like racquetball but better.

LARRY. Is it really better? I mean our lives. Yours and mine?

LORAINE. I'm having a wonderful time, aren't you?

LARRY. Yes, very much.

LORAINE. Good, that's settled. A wonderful time for everyone!

LARRY. Don't you think we should take some time and examine ourselves closely, Loraine? I mean...who are we? What are we really doing here? I mean, we hide out in this hotel room like fugitives from—

LORAINE. What are we, amoebae under a microscope here?

LARRY. I mean, we don't love each other, do we?

LORAINE. What a thing to say! Of course we don't love each other. That's the whole point.

LARRY. We like each other.

LORAINE. We don't hate each other.

LARRY. No, of course we don't hate each other, but I don't feel right.

LORAINE. Don't feel right? See a doctor.

LARRY. About us.

LORAINE *(sensing where this discussion is heading)*. It's not easy to make time for us, you know?

LARRY. I know. I'm grateful, but this—

LORAINE. I make it sound easy and look easy but it's not easy.

LARRY. I'm sure it's—

LORAINE. I tell Dorine that I'm off to see my aunt Luella for a late lunch but Dorine always asks for a telephone number in case the boss needs the numbers.

LARRY. Loraine, you've been—

LORAINE. But I tell the bitch that I'll be back by 3:30 with the damn numbers all in a row because I am good with the numbers, Larry, and I am good with you, and don't you ever forget it, do you hear me?

LARRY. We're hiding from life, Loraine!

LORAINE. Of course we're hiding from life! Why do you think we're here? I don't want truth when I'm with you, Larry. I want passion, sex, sounds! There was no passion today, Larry.

LARRY. Yeah, I'm sorry about that.

LORAINE. No sex, Larry, and no sounds...except for your snoring.

LARRY. I love Michelle.

LORAINE *(beat)*. You love Michelle.

LARRY. Yes. I mean you're wonderful...our talks at work, our takeout Chinese. *(Beat.)* I'm hurting myself here. And you. And Michelle.

LORAINE *(trying to save face)*. I sat on the end of this bed in my bra and panties waiting for you to come through that door! And when you show up you just keel over face down and take a nap! Numbers don't let you down the way people do, Larry.

LARRY. Loraine, I didn't mean to—

DORIS *(from offstage)*. Rise and shine, Larry. Time to get up.

LORAINE. So, what about next Wednesday? Want to try again?

LARRY. Look, I don't think—

LORAINE. 1:30 sharp. Yes or no?

LARRY. I've got to see my parents about—

LORAINE. You're going to tell your parents about us!

DORIS *(from offstage)*. Larry!

LARRY. Of course not, I'm just—

LORAINE *(overlapping)*. Fine! Tell the whole world! Just don't expect me to be waiting for you!

(LORAINE begins to exit, the towel in hand, and bumps into DORIS who is entering with coffee and a full breakfast. LORAINE turns to LARRY.)

LORAINE. Room service! You never ordered room service before! *(LORAINE exits.)*

DORIS. It's getting crowded around here. Who was that? Do you think she wants any breakfast?

LARRY. Mom! No. We're fine here.

DORIS. You're wrong there, son. No one's fine anymore. We're all trying to bail out the boat. *(DORIS gives the food tray to LARRY and throws open the "curtains." Rich sunlight streams into the room.)* Look at that, will you! Bursting through my window with all that cheery energy mocking me. "You're still alive, Doris?" And I stare right back and say "Hell, yes, I'm still alive. What are you going to do about it?" Of course, some days I just hide under the covers and cry. *(Looking at the array of books everywhere and beginning to pick them up.)* Will you look at all this! Read some good books, did you? Learn anything? There's not much time left.

LARRY. I tried. Didn't get much sleep.

DORIS. Well, pancakes, eggs over easy, bacon, coffee and an English muffin should put you right on course. Don't dawdle, son. This is the first day of the rest of your life. Make the best of it. *(As DORIS exits.)* I miss the sixties!

(We hear MUSIC. LIGHTS come up on the "living room" area. The stage has been cleaned of the chaos we saw at the end of Act One. SPARKY is "conducting" Tchaikovsky's "1812 Overture."*)*

SPARKY. Morning, son.

LARRY. Morning, Dad.

SPARKY *(referring to the music).* Tchaikovsky's "1812 Overture." Almost through the alphabet. Can't wait until I hit Wagner. That'll take some doing.

LARRY. Dad, can we talk a bit now?

SPARKY *(still conducting)*. Gets the blood boiling though, doesn't it? Those wacky Russians! Blood always has to keep boiling. Remember that.

LARRY. I will. Thanks.

SPARKY. Sleep well?

LARRY. Not really.

SPARKY. Good. Neither did I. If I didn't sleep well, why should you? Just joking.

LARRY. Dad? Could you please turn that down! Dad! *(The MUSIC stops.)* Sorry. Just can't concentrate. All those books! I couldn't get a handle on anything last night...and then Kevin came in and—he's a terrific kid, isn't he? Intelligent. Quick. Funny as all get out. We were having a good time and then I turned into a father and started playing "I know what's good for you, son" and he pulled away and... then I had this nightmare about...well, you don't need to know about that. Life's a jumble, Dad, isn't it?

SPARKY *(with unusual clarity)*. I don't know what to tell you, son. You're reasonably intelligent, your mother and I didn't beat you when you were a child, did we?

LARRY. No, sir. Not once.

SPARKY. I never told you to stick your head up your ass and contemplate your navel. Did I?

LARRY. No, sir. I would have remembered that.

SPARKY. Work hard, isn't that what I said?

LARRY. Yes, sir, you did and I'm trying—

SPARKY. Be fair when you can...

LARRY. Yes, sir—

SPARKY. But be brutal when you have to.

LARRY. Brutal? You never said anything about being brutal, Dad.

SPARKY. I'm sorry. I should have, but it sounded so brutal.

LARRY. I'm just trying to do it right. It's like we're back at the state championship and—

SPARKY. And you're at the plate! Bases loaded!

LARRY. And everyone is calling for a home run! *(SPARKY provides the requisite crowd chant "Lar-ry, Lar-ry, Lar-ry!")* Yeah, like that. And I'm swinging at everything that crosses the plate.

SPARKY. Actually you're swinging at a few that are way off to the…

LARRY. And I strike out!

SPARKY. Yeah, that's what you did.

LARRY. I let everybody down.

SPARKY. Just get a hit, son. Don't swing for the fence. But it's crunch time, Larry. The count's two strikes and a lot of fouls against you. You're in deep Do, son, and we're in the last act here, so suck down your mother's soggy pancakes and we'll bait up this sausage for the fish.

LARRY. Dad, I never really liked fishing very much.

SPARKY. I know that, son. But I do. And I'm driving the bus. *(Calling offstage.)* Mother? We're all set. Time to catch the whale and save the world!

(During the rest of SPARKY's speech, DORIS appears with waders, rain gear, and fishing hats. SPARKY and LARRY suit up for the fishing expedition.)

SPARKY. After we bob up and down on the water and share some quality time, we'll make a quick pit-stop to see Doctor Doom. Grab my ankles, check the old prostate…now there's a change of pace for you…thump the back a few times…cough twice to my left…I think he likes that part… then swing by the realtors and drop off the keys to—

LARRY. Leave them with me, Dad! I'll look after the house. Paint the stairs, maybe. Fix the old trim over the door.

SPARKY. You're too busy, son.

DORIS. You have your own life to mend, Larry. What's left of it.

SPARKY. Then off to the travel office to scoop up those tickets and Katmandu, here we come!

LARRY. Stop, please. This is all so fast. Let me help. I want to feel useful. Please. Everything's falling down around me.

DORIS. Of course it is, son. Stability's an illusion.

SPARKY. It's all done with mirrors and smoke screens.

DORIS. Reality's nothing but chaos.

SPARKY. Remember, your future's either half full or half empty, son.

DORIS. In your case, it's mostly empty right now.

SPARKY. Well done, Mother. We can check off that quality moment. Now...*(SPARKY seems distracted.)*...where did I leave that rowboat?

DORIS *(to LARRY confidentially)*. These witty "truisms" are going to be the death of me. Keep an eye on your father. All his muffins ain't rising in the oven this morning. *(Calling offstage.)* Could you bring on the rowboat, Please!

(LIGHTS come up on another area of the stage as we see the PROPS ASSISTANT bring on a "rowboat" shell.)

DORIS. Look, Sparky. Sweetheart, there it is. Exactly where you left it.

SPARKY *(like a general of war calling for his weapons)*. Fishing poles! Hurry, hurry. Time and tide wait for hardly anyone, remember that!

(The PROPS ASSISTANT reappears with fishing poles in hand.)

SPARKY. Bait! Tackle. Guard. Center. Hurry!

(The PROPS ASSISTANT exits quickly and then returns with a bait pail.)

SPARKY. Come on, son! I can hear 'em biting now! *(SPARKY and LARRY begin to get into the boat.)*

DORIS. Wait a minute. *(Calling offstage.)* Kevin? *(To LARRY.)* You can't leave people behind in your life, son. They'll think they're not important.

(KEVIN appears. He looks distinctly unenthusiastic.)

KEVIN. I don't want to go fishing! The guys are waiting for me. Somebody give me some keys! Grandma, can I have your—

DORIS. Young man, get in there and have a good time with your elders or I'll box your ears.

KEVIN *(getting into the "rowboat")*. This is stupid! I never catch anything anyway.

DORIS. Wait a minute! We've forgotten—

(The PROPS ASSISTANT appears with an armload of fishing gear for KEVIN. The ASSISTANT also brings three sack lunches.)

PROPS ASSISTANT. I've got it! I've got it! What you would all do without me, I can't imagine! *(Tossing them the sack lunches.)* Some dried bologna sandwiches, potato salad with too much mustard, dill pickles and some Cheetos.

DORIS. Oh, what a picture! I wish I had a—*(The ASSISTANT whips out a camera and quickly snaps several pictures then tosses the camera to DORIS who looks closely at the ASSISTANT.)* Have we met before?

PROPS ASSISTANT *(exiting)*. What a family! Three vacuum cleaners, television sets everywhere, and those Elvis Presley Commemorative...*(He's gone.)*

DORIS. OK! Have a great time! Fire in the belly, and all that. Be back by 4:30. Bye! *(DORIS waves. Ad libs all around. KEVIN looks trapped, LARRY looks disoriented, and SPARKY prepares to fish. LIGHTS fade down on the "rowboat" as the MEN "freeze" in their respective fishing postures. LIGHTS now favor DORIS who calls offstage.)* All clear! They've gone. What a sight.

(A moment later MICHELLE enters.)

DORIS. You know? I wouldn't be a man for all the tea in China.

MICHELLE. Will they be all right? The sky looks cloudy.

DORIS. Who cares? This isn't Golden Pond, dear. They'll be all right. They're just in a "freeze" over there. See them? Don't they look strange? They'll be back. But right now there's a little time for us. Care for some tea?

MICHELLE. Thank you, yes, that would be wonderful.

DORIS *(calling offstage)*. Cheeves, would you come here a moment, please?

(DORIS and MICHELLE move to the "living room" where CHEEVES, dressed smartly in a butler's tux and tails, brings out a second chair for MICHELLE.)

CHEEVES. Yes, madam?

DORIS. Tea if you please, Cheeves. And there's some Sara Lee in the refrigerator.

CHEEVES. Very good, madam. *(CHEEVES exits but not before winking at DORIS.)*

MICHELLE. He winked at you!

DORIS. Fantasies are wonderful, aren't they? And harmless. They make us feel so alive. He's one of my better creations. Did you see his hands? So strong, so…never mind, we're here to get down and dirty. You first.

MICHELLE. Well, I don't really know where to begin.

DORIS. Start somewhere toward the end, sweetie. I've got a big day ahead of me.

MICHELLE. I'm unhappy.

DORIS. OK. That's a start. And?

MICHELLE. And what?

DORIS. Happiness isn't a birthright. You didn't know that, did you? It's not like getting coupons in the mail. Now that's a birthright!

MICHELLE. I don't think we're going to make it. I don't think we're going to survive. We've lost a sense of togetherness. We don't eat meals together, we don't talk with each other…just "tell" things to each other like "I'll be at this number" or "I'm working late tonight" or "It's your turn to pick up the laundry."

DORIS. Sounds like a marriage to me.

MICHELLE. Get this, buy that, gimme this, gotta have that! God!

DORIS. Are you going to scream again?

MICHELLE. I'd like to.

KEVIN. Hey, Mom, look at what I caught!

(LIGHTS come up on the three MEN. LARRY seems to be holding his own, SPARKY is still fumbling with his gear, and KEVIN is holding up a small fish he has caught.)

DORIS. Oh, look. There they are. The great white fishermen. Yoo-hoo! *(DORIS and MICHELLE wave.)*

SPARKY *(launching into a fractured selection from* Moby Dick*)*. Thar she blows, maties! A hump like a snow-hill! It's Moby Dick! Man the mastheads! Get the son-of-a-bitch! Where's that bologna sandwich! *(DORIS throws SPARKY a kiss as the LIGHTS again fade down on the MEN.)*

DORIS. So, where were we? Oh, yes. The marriage is collapsing, Kevin is a delinquent, Larry is going flaccid, metaphorically speaking, and you're spending your mornings in the Safeway screaming your head off. Doesn't sound like the best of times to me.

MICHELLE. It's terrible. I don't think it's supposed to be this way.

DORIS. Not like the movies, is it?

(CHEEVES enters with tea and the cake.)

DORIS. Isn't that right, Cheeves?

CHEEVES. What's that, madam?

DORIS. That life has nothing to do with art. With fiction. That life is...well, life!

CHEEVES. Very good, madam. Will that be all?

DORIS. Yes, thank you, Cheeves. *(CHEEVES blows DORIS a kiss, then exits.)* Isn't he a wonder, though? Such strong hands.

MICHELLE. Why do you do that?

DORIS. Do what?

MICHELLE. Flirt with him.

DORIS. To feel the energy, I suppose. The excitement of breaking out of the harness for a moment or two.

MICHELLE. I think I'm going to take a lover.

DORIS. Oh, this is juicy. Damaging, destructive, and humiliating, but juicy. Where are you taking him?

(As if sensing that something important is transpiring that intimately affects him, LARRY "comes alive" in the rowboat. KEVIN and SPARKY remain in their "freeze" postures.)

LARRY. A lover? Oh, Jesus.

MICHELLE. I don't want to. But I need someone to show me some…make me feel I'm…

DORIS. Desired? Needed?

MICHELLE. Yes.

LARRY *(to MICHELLE who remains unaware of his "presence")*. I need you, Michelle!

DORIS. Someone who will listen and hold you.

MICHELLE. Yes.

DORIS. And all you have to do is take your pleasure and then walk out the door.

MICHELLE. It sounds so—

DORIS. Don't do it.

MICHELLE. But Larry hurt me. And I'm…I want to…

DORIS. And you want to hurt him back.

MICHELLE. Yes.

DORIS. Did he mean to?

LARRY. No!

MICHELLE. Does it matter?

DORIS. Sometimes. You think it's what you need, what you want, but it's not. I thought the same thing with Fred.

MICHELLE. Fred?

LARRY. Fred? Who's Fred? *(To SPARKY.)* Dad, did you know anything about a Fred? *(SPARKY remains in his posture.)*

DORIS. When Larry was just a child we didn't have much money. Sparky worked two jobs. These were the old days and the mother stayed at home. Then Larry got scarlet fever and the hospital bills were...Sparky took a third job. I hardly ever saw him. I'd have dinner on the table and it would sit there for hours.

MICHELLE. You must have felt—

DORIS. Very alone. I wanted Sparky there. With me. With Larry.

MICHELLE. Who was Fred?

DORIS. Fred lived next door. He came over to sit with me. His wife suffered from depression and we would listen to each other's problems. What channel is this on?

MICHELLE. What happened? Please.

DORIS. We held each other. It felt good. I was tempted. But it scared me, too. It was very easy. That night I told Sparky I needed him in my heart, and if he didn't need me the same way he could take out the trash on his way out the door. I've had his attention ever since.

LARRY. What did he say, Mom?

DORIS. He put his arms around me and said life was immense, uncontrollable, that he was exhausted.

LARRY. He was trying to keep it all together.

MICHELLE. And what about me? Can't I be exhausted, too? I'm very angry at him.

DORIS. When men can't...tack down all the edges, dear... they flop around like fish out of water. It's not a pretty sight.

MICHELLE. Then what happened?

DORIS. We started kissing and he swept everything off the dining room table and we—

(At this moment KEVIN displays several new fish.)

KEVIN. Look at me, Dad. They're just jumping into the boat!

(SPARKY unfreezes.)

SPARKY. Hey, Big Guy, that's quite a haul there! *(SPARKY, KEVIN and LARRY provide supportive ad libs.)*

DORIS. Well, that was my Sally Jessy Raphael moment. How did I—*(DORIS suddenly buckles over in pain. LARRY's focus is directed toward KEVIN and SPARKY.)* Ooohh...

MICHELLE. Doris, what's wrong? Are you—

DORIS. Oh, damn. I thought maybe this wouldn't happen now...*(Again she is hit with a sharp pain.)*

MICHELLE. What's the matter?

DORIS. The doctor's not sure what it is. Sparky doesn't know.

MICHELLE. You need help.

DORIS. There's no time. Sparky's been looking forward to—

MICHELLE *(overlapping and shouting in the direction of the MEN who remain intent on their fishing)*. Larry! Larry! Sparky! Kevin! Someone! Please!

(THE DOCTOR appears from the wings.)

THE DOCTOR. Those pains again, Doris?

MICHELLE *(overlapping)*. We were just talking and she bent over and—*(THE DOCTOR assists DORIS offstage.)* Wait, where are you taking her? *(MICHELLE calls to LARRY one last time then exits after DORIS. LIGHTS fully favor the MEN.)*

SPARKY. Isn't this the life, though? The bubbling waters, the warm sun on your brow, a day fishing with the guys. Doesn't get any better than this.

KEVIN. Who brought the beer?

LARRY. Kevin.

KEVIN. Hey, just trying to get into the spirit of things.

LARRY. Tough break about the fish, Dad.

SPARKY. Oh, that's OK. It's really all about the bubbling waters, the warm sun on your brow—*(LARRY nods to KEVIN that he should give his fish to SPARKY.)*

KEVIN. I'll give you mine if you want, Granddad?

SPARKY. No, no! I couldn't. To the victor go the spoils. Those are the rules.

KEVIN. What do we do with 'em, anyway?

SPARKY. Well, I thought you and your dad could fry 'em up in the back yard, create a big mess and have a lot of fun.

LARRY *(to KEVIN)*. Yeah, and we can spend a few nights in the pup tent, then work on Granddad's front porch and—

KEVIN. Na, can't. Got things to do. Can we go now?

LARRY. Hey, can't we spend some time together...maybe just...aw, hell.

SPARKY *(after a tense moment or two, attempting to play the "with it" grandfather)*. So, what's up these days with you kids?

KEVIN. Nothin' much, Granddad.

SPARKY. Come on, fill me in. What's "goin' down!" Got a girlfriend?

KEVIN. Well, uh...yeah, I guess.

SPARKY. What's her name? Bobbie, Joannie, Holly?

KEVIN. Heather.

SPARKY. Heather. Now that's a pretty name. Sounds like a cologne.

LARRY. Heather? Have I met Heather? You haven't mentioned a Heather before.

KEVIN. You never asked.

LARRY. Invite her over. Your mom and I like to meet your friends.

KEVIN. She's just one of the gang, Dad. It's no big deal.

SPARKY *(to KEVIN)*. That's just father stuff. We've got to ask all those questions. You will, too. You become a father and you get a pamphlet in the mail. "Twenty Things Every Father Has to Say to His Kids." I couldn't get your dad to bring his girlfriends home for dinner either.

KEVIN. Girlfriends! Dad had girlfriends!

LARRY. Yes, I had girlfriends!

SPARKY. I remember one night I heard the garage door slide up. Must have been almost midnight. He didn't want me to know he was there.

KEVIN. But you heard him.

SPARKY. Yep, 'cause I had ears of steel. So I lean out the window and say "Who's that?" And he says "It's OK, Dad. It's just me." And there was a woman with him.

KEVIN. In the garage?

SPARKY. So I say, "Who's that with you, son?"

(LIGHTS come up on MICHELLE who looks more relaxed than we've seen her. There's a freshness about her. KEVIN watches this "replay" with considerable interest.)

MICHELLE. "Hello. My name's Michelle."

SPARKY. "That's a pretty name."

MICHELLE. "Thank you."

SPARKY. "Two 'll's' or one?"

MICHELLE. "Two. Two 'll's.' "

KEVIN. Is this a memory thing?

LARRY. I was taking a German class at UCLA. The summer after I graduated from college. I'd gotten an ROTC commission and was going on active duty.

SPARKY *(to KEVIN)*. He was heading for Germany.

LARRY. I wanted to learn a bit of the language. It was a big adventure for me.

MICHELLE. I was going to Heidelberg to study European history. I thought I wanted to become a teacher.

LARRY. She was sitting a few seats in front of me in class.

MICHELLE. I could tell you were watching me.

LARRY. How?

MICHELLE. I get this little tickle on my neck whenever someone stares at me.

KEVIN. Maybe it's a skin rash, Mom. *(SPARKY quiets KEVIN.)*

LARRY. And I asked her if she'd like a ride home after class.

MICHELLE. I said yes. *(LARRY steps out of the "rowboat" and joins MICHELLE.)*

SPARKY. Your dad had left his car in the garage so they walked back to the house.

MICHELLE. We talked all the way.

LARRY. You thought I was funny.

KEVIN. Dad's not very funny, Mom.

MICHELLE. He used to be. He made me laugh a lot. *(Looking at LARRY.)* And we talked about college, and the world, and travel, and money, and parents, and children and life after death. And I fell in love with you. *(KEVIN is caught up in watching his parents behave like people.)*

SPARKY. And I told him to drive carefully, put on the emergency break, and be home at a reasonable hour.

KEVIN. He was out of college, Granddad!

SPARKY. It's in the pamphlet, Kevin. You're a parent for life!

MICHELLE. And he came to Heidelberg—

LARRY. And we married—*(This section is both a remembrance and an offering, a testing to see if they are still connected enough to make the marriage work.)*

MICHELLE. And we traveled to Paris—

LARRY. And Rome—

MICHELLE *(to KEVIN)*. And then we came home and had you.

KEVIN. Thanks

MICHELLE. And things were good. Very good.

LARRY. Good job, good house.

MICHELLE. Lots of friends. Laughter.

LARRY. Cookouts. Sunsets.

MICHELLE. And then things got…

LARRY. Busy…

MICHELLE. Frantic—

LARRY. Stressful—

MICHELLE *(to LARRY)*. You were never at home—

LARRY. There was overtime, planes to catch, reports to write—

MICHELLE *(to KEVIN)*. And then you started getting older.

LARRY. Braces, glasses—

MICHELLE. Boy Scouts, ten-speed bikes—

LARRY. Toys, computers—

KEVIN. I'm sorry, OK?

LARRY. No, no, son. It wasn't your fault.

MICHELLE. We love you.

LARRY. Always will. It was just—

MICHELLE. Things, and time—

LARRY. Getting older—

MICHELLE. My part-time job—

LARRY. Then promotions and more overtime, and more reports—

MICHELLE. Then my full-time job—

LARRY. And I thought I was going to drown.

MICHELLE. Then my first drink.

KEVIN. I see the bottles in the trash. Out back.

MICHELLE. I'm sorry for that, Kevin.

LARRY. Then the spending, "things" would make it all worth while.

MICHELLE. Cars, blow dryers, cashmere sweaters, designer this and designer that.

LARRY. Time shares we didn't have time for, golf bags I never used.

MICHELLE. And lights that go on when you clap your hands.

LARRY. And lights that go off when you clap your hands…

MICHELLE. Then my second drink.

KEVIN. Ah, Mom.

SPARKY. You lose track of yourself, Kevin. You make mistakes. No one means to.

KEVIN. I won't!

SPARKY. Yes, you will, Kevin. It's part of the trip.

(THE LOVER enters.)

THE LOVER. Hi. Ready? Miss me?

LARRY. Ready? Ready for what? Who is this man, Michelle?

THE LOVER. I'm the lover, Jack. The office lover. She mentioned me earlier.

LARRY. My name's not Jack.

THE LOVER. Does it matter? *(To MICHELLE.)* Are you ready? You look terrific.

LARRY. Michelle, what's all this about?

MICHELLE. He just started listening to me one day, Larry. We had things in common.

THE LOVER. Reports, and meetings, and cappuccino in the afternoon.

MICHELLE. And he cared.

LARRY. Ready for what? What are you going to do?

THE LOVER. We're on the empowerment team at the office. She's the team leader. It's very empowering.

LARRY. What team is that? I didn't know you were the head of a—

THE LOVER. She came up with the cost reduction plan that saved the company—

LARRY *(to THE LOVER)*. Why don't you get the hell out of here? You're not going anywhere with my wife! And you don't have to tell me about Michelle's abilities. She's wonderful. She's always been—

MICHELLE. Larry, please. This isn't about you.

LARRY. Not about me! What do you mean this isn't about me!

MICHELLE. I have to work things out for myself.

LARRY. You're going off with some guy to…a hotel room to—

LORAINE *(offstage)*. Larry?

(LIGHTS come up on LORAINE.)

LORAINE. Larry? I've just got two more calls to make then I'll be free.

MICHELLE. Is that your friend, Larry? Your "lunch" friend?

LARRY. Michelle, don't go with him.

MICHELLE. She is, isn't she?

LARRY. It's a big mistake. You'll feel worse. I know.

LORAINE. Larry, you go ahead. I've made the reservations. All is forgiven.

LARRY *(to MICHELLE)*. I was wrong, Michelle. I love you. Please don't—

KEVIN. Who's that, Dad?

LARRY. She works with me at the office, Kevin. Please!

KEVIN. Can I get a job there?

SPARKY. This isn't funny, young man. This is deadly serious. This isn't a movie.

(LIGHTS come up revealing DORIS hooked up to a portable I.V. unit.)

DORIS. Oh, you've started without me again. I hate it when you do that. What have I missed?

SPARKY. Mother? Good God, what's happened? *(We hear "Mom, you OK?" "Grandma, why are you—?" And so on.)*

DORIS. It's OK now. Michelle and I were having a nice little talk about marriage and infidelity and all of a sudden this pain...*(To THE LOVER.)* And who are you, young man?

THE LOVER. I'm Michelle's wannabe office lover.

DORIS. Oh, dear. Yes, I bet you are.

SPARKY *(pointing to LORAINE)*. And that woman there is Larry's "friend."

LORAINE. And I'm very good at—

DORIS *(to LORAINE)*. Spare me the details, thank you. I get the picture...*(To LARRY.)* You're living in a soap opera here, Larry. Get a grip.

THE LOVER. Hey, this family stuff makes me cuddly all over, but time's moving on. I've got things to do.

LORAINE. So do I, Larry. I have to get the numbers in by 3:30.

THE LOVER. Michelle, you'll love the room, it's—

KEVIN. Mom?

LARRY. Michelle. Don't. Stay here and talk with me, please.

THE LOVER. I can't wait any longer, Michelle. I have a busy schedule.

SPARKY *(to THE LOVER)*. Don't let us keep you, fella!

KEVIN. Dad, don't you love Mom?

LARRY. Yes, son. I do. Every second. Every—

MICHELLE. Then what's wrong with me, Larry? We never talk. You don't hold me anymore.

LARRY. Nothing's wrong with you. It's me. I felt I had to provide everything for everyone!

THE LOVER. Look, this confessional stuff is all—

LARRY. And I couldn't do it! And then I looked in the mirror and I didn't like who I saw there and I got frightened. I wanted to hide.

LORAINE. That's why I'm here, Larry. So you don't have to look in the mirror.

THE LOVER. Frightened? Aw, give me a break.

SPARKY. It's crunch time, son. Bases loaded.

DORIS. She wants to feel safe again, Larry.

THE LOVER. Hey, I can make her feel safe. My calendar's her calendar.

LARRY *(to THE LOVER)*. I told you to butt out of—

THE LOVER. There's a lot of energy around the water cooler, Jack. You don't take care of business someone else'll take care of it for you.

LARRY. My name's not Jack! *(LARRY hauls off and slugs THE LOVER who staggers back out of the scene. LARRY nurses his hand.)*

KEVIN. Nice hit, Pop.

SPARKY. I taught him how to box in the garage when he was eleven.

LORAINE. What about me, Larry? Time's running out. *(EVERYONE looks at LARRY.)*

LARRY. I'm sorry, Loraine. No more lunches. No more afternoon reservations.

LORAINE. Is that a decision, Larry? Did you actually make a decision? Are you going to hit me, too?

LARRY. It's nothing against you, Loraine. It's just not right for me.

LORAINE *(to MICHELLE)*. Well, you can have him, honey. He never had his heart in it anyway. *(To LARRY.)* Come to think of it, most times you never had your—

DORIS. It was nice meeting you, young lady. Good-bye! *(LIGHTS fade out on LORAINE.)*

MICHELLE *(to LARRY)*. Are you all right?

LARRY. No, I don't think so. What a...are you OK?

MICHELLE. No.

LARRY. I've made some big mistakes, Michelle, haven't I?

MICHELLE. Yes, you have. Very big.

LARRY. Have you? Have you made any big mistakes?

MICHELLE. Yes. *(Beat.)* But not as big as yours.

KEVIN. You adults really screw things up, don't you?

SPARKY. It's a jungle out here, Kevin. You can't see the forest for the trees sometimes. It looks like a lake, but it's really a jungle.

DORIS *(feeling a twinge of pain in her stomach)*. Oooh. Sparky, dear?

SPARKY. Oh, sweetheart! Are you all right? *(EVERYONE gathers around DORIS.)*

DORIS. I had to take some tests, that's all.

SPARKY. Tests? I thought you graduated years ago.

(THE DOCTOR enters carrying a clipboard and thumbing through some test results.)

THE DOCTOR. Sparky, old sport. You look good. I never see this end of you. Catch anything this time? Still reading *Moby Dick*?

SPARKY *(to THE DOCTOR)*. You're making a house call? This'll cost me an arm and a leg! *(To DORIS.)* What happened? I'm supposed to be the sick one.

DORIS. Cheeves kept throwing kisses to me and then—

SPARKY. Kisses? What kisses?

DORIS. This pain hit me in the stomach.

SPARKY. What pain? You've never told me about—

THE DOCTOR. She's been working too hard. Lots of worry. You're not sharing the wear, Sparky.

DORIS. He says we should take it easy. Cancel the trip maybe.

SPARKY. Cancel the trip? You mean this is it? The party's over? No Peking opera?

LARRY. Dad, don't get—

SPARKY. But there's a new *Star Trek* coming out and I was going to test drive the new Blazer 6000!

LARRY. Mom didn't say your life was over, Dad. Take it easy.

SPARKY. I know that, son. But life's not about taking it easy. Never forget that. Can't just sit around with your thumbs up your…gotta live!

KEVIN. Get off the dime.

SPARKY. Get with the program.

KEVIN. Get your butt in gear!

SPARKY. Shape up or ship out.

KEVIN. Don't screw the pooch.

THE DOCTOR. No pain, no gain.

SPARKY *(to THE DOCTOR)*. You should know.

LARRY. Doctor, please, what actually seems to be—

THE DOCTOR. I think I need to run some more tests. One Quadro plasty, a full blood slate and a Jiffy Lube. There's a special this month. Seriously, nothing terminal. Just wear and tear. Comes with the territory. But I just want to be sure.

MICHELLE. I'm so sorry, Doris.

DORIS. I was looking forward to room service.

SPARKY. The Eiffel Tower. St. Peter's.

DORIS. More room service.

THE DOCTOR. Well, you can go next year. Maybe.

LARRY. What do you mean…maybe?

THE DOCTOR *(to LARRY)*. You only have so many miles on the tires, you know.

SPARKY *(to THE DOCTOR)*. You have a delightful bedside manner, did anyone ever tell you that before?

DORIS. He's right, Sparky. *(To THE DOCTOR.)* Nothing terminal, right?

THE DOCTOR. Well, yes, but I might find something that—

DORIS. And you might not, right?

THE DOCTOR. Now wait a minute, I can always find something!

DORIS. Well, you can find something later. *(DORIS detaches the I.V. unit from her arm. Ad libs of concern all around.)* Oh, don't worry. It's a symbolic gesture. This is a play. We taped it down backstage. *(To THE DOCTOR.)* Take this with you on your way out, and if I need it when we get back I'll hook it up again. And if we don't get back, then who cares! We're going!

SPARKY. Going? Where are we going now?

THE DOCTOR. She's right, Sparky. You only go around once. In a couple of months you'll be hale and hearty…or you won't. Only time will tell. Either way, take two aspirin and pay me in the morning. See ya. *(As THE DOCTOR exits.)* I love that line.

SPARKY. If we don't get back! What do you mean if we don't get—

MICHELLE. You're all packed, Sparky.

LARRY. The world at your fingertips, Dad.

MICHELLE. Don't you want to go?

SPARKY. Of course I want to go, but what about the three of you?

DORIS. They have to work it out for themselves, Sparky, the way we all have to. *(The SOUND of a cruise ship horn is heard.)* Hurry up, we don't have much time.

LARRY. Go ahead, Dad. We'll be fine. At least we'll try to be fine...well, we'll try and do something. Maybe on the weekends we'll all bunk in here. I can help out with the cooking.

DORIS. Don't push it, son.

SPARKY. You and Kevin can fix the front porch together.

LARRY. What do you say, Kevin?

KEVIN. You going to pay me?

LARRY *(beat)*. No.

KEVIN *(beat)*. Well...if you're going to cook, I want dessert first.

SPARKY. Sold! Everything you need's in the shed! That was close. Been wanting to get that porch fixed for years.

DORIS. Oh, darn! I never fixed your favorite chocolate cake, son.

LARRY. Mom, it's OK. Really.

DORIS. Sparky, hurry!

MICHELLE. Kevin, give us a hand. *(MICHELLE and KEVIN help DORIS with the luggage.)*

DORIS *(exiting)*. Kevin, if your father's going to cook, there's a Domino's number on the fridge.

SPARKY *(putting on his coat and making preparations to exit)*. Well, son, good luck with your life. We've done all we can. Your mother and I are off! Guess we've made that abundantly clear, haven't we?

LARRY. Dad, did you know about...I mean, did Mom ever... I don't want to do the wrong thing here.

SPARKY. No one on this earth walks on water, son. At least not yet. Just get on base. Don't swing for the fence. Listen to your heart.

(MICHELLE and KEVIN re-enter. SPARKY has now gathered up a few luggage pieces in his arms and pauses to give LARRY a final piece of advice.)

SPARKY. The mirrors, son. Take the mirrors off the walls. They'll scare you to death!

DORIS *(from offstage)*. Sparky!

SPARKY *(exiting)*. Thar she blows! Kevin, get the door.

(KEVIN helps SPARKY exit. LARRY and MICHELLE remain on the stage. After an extended moment KEVIN re-enters.)

KEVIN. Well, they're off. *(Beat.)* Sure is quiet. *(Everyone is uncertain how to interact. KEVIN pokes around in the gear LARRY brought in at the beginning of the play.)*

LARRY *(to MICHELLE)*. How do you bake a cake?

MICHELLE. Read the recipe on the back of the box.

LARRY. Not too difficult.

MICHELLE. Nope.

LARRY *(referring now to their relationship)*. This is going to be harder, isn't it?

MICHELLE. Much harder.

LARRY. No recipe on the marriage box.

MICHELLE. Right.

LARRY. Do you want to try? *(KEVIN watches his parents intently.)*

MICHELLE. Maybe. I don't know if I've got any energy left.

LARRY. We'll find some. We'll make some.

KEVIN. What are we going to do now? I'm hungry.

LARRY. You're going to finish school.

KEVIN. Right now? I meant—

LARRY. And mow the lawn and sit down to dinner with your mother and me. If she'll have me back.

KEVIN. If it doesn't work can I leave?

MICHELLE *(believing LARRY's sincerity).* One step at a time, OK.

LARRY *(beat).* Right. OK. So, hungry, eh? What do you say I whip up some grub in the kitchen and—

MICHELLE. Where's that Domino's number, Kevin?

KEVIN. Call it in, Mom, and I'll go get it...*(Pulling out SPARKY's car keys.)* I've got Granddad's car keys.

LARRY. Oh, no!

KEVIN. He said it was now or never. Back in ten minutes. *(KEVIN exits. MICHELLE and LARRY take a few tentative steps toward each other.)*

LARRY. Hi.

MICHELLE. Hello.

LARRY. I've been watching you in class.

MICHELLE. I know.

END OF PLAY

CHARACTER NOTES

- SPARKY: Gregarious, high-spirited, tends to lose his focus now and then
- DORIS: A no-nonsense, down-to-earth woman who calls 'em as she sees 'em
- LARRY: Intelligent but finding himself overwhelmed by the tempo and complexity of his life
- MICHELLE: Senses that she, too, is at a crossroads
- KEVIN: Sharp-minded but caught in the turbulence of adolescence
- LORAINE: A hard-driving middle-management colleague
- THE BOSS: Supercilious
- TRAVEL AGENT: Seductive, subtle

DIRECTOR'S NOTES

DIRECTOR'S NOTES

DIRECTOR'S NOTES

DIRECTOR'S NOTES

DIRECTOR'S NOTES

DIRECTOR'S NOTES